Re

This
belo
tele

OVERCOMING YOUR ADDICTIONS

DR WINDY DRYDEN was born in London in 1950. He has worked in psychotherapy and counselling for more than twenty-five years. Dr Dryden is the author or editor of more than 120 books, including *How to Accept Yourself* (Sheldon Press, 1999) and *Overcoming Anxiety* (Sheldon Press, 2000). He is Professor of Counselling at Goldsmiths College, University of London.

DR WALTER MATWEYCHUK was educated at the University of Pennsylvania (BA, MS) and Hofstra University (MA, PhD). Trained by Dr Albert Ellis, the founder of Rational Emotive Behavior Therapy, he has practised psychotherapy for ten years, helping adults to overcome various behavioural problems. Dr Matweychuk enjoys regular physical exercise and has been a finisher in the New York City Marathon for the past ten years. He lives in Manhattan, New York, with his wife Pamela.

Overcoming Common Problems Series

For a full list of titles please contact
Sheldon Press, Marylebone Road, London NW1 4DU

Antioxidants
DR ROBERT YOUNGSON

The Assertiveness Workbook
A plan for busy women
JOANNA GUTMANN

Beating the Comfort Trap
DR WINDY DRYDEN AND JACK
GORDON

Body Language
How to read others' thoughts by their
gestures
ALLAN PEASE

Body Language in Relationships
DAVID COHEN

Calm Down
How to cope with frustration and anger
DR PAUL HAUCK

Cancer – A Family Affair
NEVILLE SHONE

The Cancer Guide for Men
HELEN BEARE AND NEIL PRIDDY

The Candida Diet Book
KAREN BRODY

Caring for Your Elderly Parent
JULIA BURTON-JONES

Cider Vinegar
MARGARET HILLS

Comfort for Depression
JANET HORWOOD

Considering Adoption?
SARAH BIGGS

Coping Successfully with Hay Fever
DR ROBERT YOUNGSON

**Coping Successfully with Joint
Replacement**
DR TOM SMITH

Coping Successfully with Migraine
SUE DYSON

Coping Successfully with Pain
NEVILLE SHONE

Coping Successfully with Panic Attacks
SHIRLEY TRICKETT

Coping Successfully with PMS
KAREN EVENNETT

**Coping Successfully with Prostate
Problems**
ROSY REYNOLDS

Coping Successfully with RSI
MAGGIE BLACK AND PENNY GRAY

**Coping Successfully with Your Hiatus
Hernia**
DR TOM SMITH

**Coping Successfully with Your Irritable
Bladder**
DR JENNIFER HUNT

**Coping Successfully with Your Irritable
Bowel**
ROSEMARY NICOL

**Coping When Your Child Has Special
Needs**
SUZANNE ASKHAM

Coping with Anxiety and Depression
SHIRLEY TRICKETT

Coping with Blushing
DR ROBERT EDELMANN

Coping with Breast Cancer
DR EADIE HEYDERMAN

Coping with Bronchitis and Emphysema
DR TOM SMITH

Coping with Candida
SHIRLEY TRICKETT

Coping with Chronic Fatigue
TRUDIE CHALDER

Coping with Coeliac Disease
KAREN BRODY

Coping with Cystitis
CAROLINE CLAYTON

Coping with Depression and Elation
DR PATRICK McKEON

Coping with Eczema
DR ROBERT YOUNGSON

Coping with Endometriosis
JO MEARS

Coping with Epilepsy
FIONA MARSHALL AND
DR PAMELA CRAWFORD

Coping with Fibroids
MARY-CLAIRE MASON

Coping with Gallstones
DR JOAN GOMEZ

Coping with Headaches and Migraine
SHIRLEY TRICKETT

Coping with a Hernia
DR DAVID DELVIN

Coping with Psoriasis
PROFESSOR RONALD MARKS

Coping with Rheumatism and Arthritis
DR ROBERT YOUNGSON

Overcoming Common Problems Series

Overcoming Common Problems Series

Overcoming Common Problems

Overcoming Your Addictions

Dr Windy Dryden
and
Dr Walter Matweychuk

sheldon **PRESS**

Declaration

To discuss the issue of addiction fully and within the context of case study, it was necessary to include among examples of addictive substances ones that at present are illegal. The publisher, Sheldon Press/SPCK, would like to make clear that such mentioning of these substances is not in any way an endorsement, by it, of the use of these substances.

First published in Great Britain in 2000 by
Sheldon Press
Holy Trinity Church
Marylebone Road
London NW1 4DU

British Library Cataloguing-in-Publication Data

A catalogue record for this book is available from the British Library

ISBN 0–85969–845–9

Typeset by Deltatype Limited, Birkenhead, Merseyside
Printed in Great Britain by
Biddles Ltd, Guildford and King's Lynn

Contents

Preface

We have written this book for those who are seriously contemplating overcoming their dependence on alcohol, drugs, junk food, cigarettes, chocolate or other myriad things, and who primarily use them to cope with the hassles and emotional pain of daily living.

We do not pretend that this book is all you need to overcome your addiction. You would do well to involve the support of friends and family and enlist the support of professionals when you need to. By all means, gain help from such groups as Alcoholics Anonymous and Narcotics Anonymous; get help from wherever you can. This book will assist you along the way towards sober and clean living, but only if you actually practise what you learn.

Overcoming addiction is difficult and no one book will contain all you need to help yourself. You may need other literature to help you deal with the disturbed emotions to which you are prone and which you have covered up with cigarettes, tranquillizers, alcohol or the like. Here are some reading suggestions.

For help with anxiety problems, read *Overcoming Anxiety* by Windy Dryden (Sheldon Press, 2000).

For help with depression, read *Overcoming Depression* by Paul Gilbert (Robinson, 1997).

For help with problems of shame and guilt, read *Overcoming Guilt* by Windy Dryden (Sheldon, 1994) and *Overcoming Shame* by Windy Dryden (Sheldon, 1997).

For help with anger problems, read *Overcoming Anger* by Windy Dryden (Sheldon, 1996).

For help with jealousy, read *Overcoming Jealousy* by Windy Dryden (Sheldon, 1999).

We hope that you find our book useful in your quest to become and stay free from addiction and invite your feedback c/o Sheldon Press.

Windy Dryden, London and East Sussex
Walter Matweychuk, New York

1

Focus on what you will gain by overcoming your addiction

People become dependent on a whole range of addictive substances – drugs, alcohol, nicotine, sleeping pills, tranquillizers, even junk food and chocolate, to name the most common examples. The first step in giving up any of these is to become aware of all the benefits that will come to you by learning how to tolerate the discomfort of daily living without resorting to the relief provided by such things as nicotine and alcohol. Although you may be somwhat aware that you would be better off if you did not use any of these, you may resist working on giving them up because you wrongly focus on all the fun, pleasure, etc., that you will be missing if you do give them up. Simultaneously you may also focus on all the difficulty, discomfort and stress you will experience in trying to give up this pleasurable activity. People who are addicted stop themselves from addressing their addiction by holding beliefs like 'It is too hard to give up all that fun and too difficult and uncomfortable to change. My life would lose all its fun and not be worth living. I could not stand that!'

Our experience has shown that to successfully give up an addiction, it is important that you train yourself to focus on all the good things which you will gain and to avoid dwelling on what you will be giving up. You may be thinking of making yet another attempt to give up the thing you are addicted to after losing a good job, getting arrested, getting into an accident and injuring yourself or someone else, becoming aware of financial or health-related problems that stem from your addiction, losing custody of your children after a divorce or experiencing some other type of painful loss. You may be beginning to be aware of how the addiction is stopping you from moving from one phase of life into another, as when a student has trouble finishing college and making a transition into their first career-related job. Whatever your motivation,

1

the more you focus on what you have to gain by overcoming your addiction rather than on what you have to lose, the more likely your attempts to help yourself will be successful.

One important thing which people who achieve a good deal of success in their lives have learned how to do is to respond to defeats and losses by learning from them and benefiting from that experience. And it is not a matter of having the 'character' or 'strength' to overcome a loss, but learning the strategies that enable you to rebound from a loss, mistake or defeat. This is not a subjective point of view; research has also shown it to be true. For example, a study once showed that a very large percentage of the individuals who had managed to give up smoking cigarettes for more than ten years without having had professional help had one very important thing in common. That was that these 'ten-year plus abstainers' had all made at least four or five previous attempts at quitting smoking before finding the 'secret' to long-term 'abstinence'. Given that an estimated many millions have given up cigarette smoking, such people are living evidence that you too can overcome your addiction if you are willing to keep working at it until you succeed! And if you stop overlooking the price you pay every day for being addicted, you will begin to feel motivated to try again!

Some of you may not believe that a person can learn skills, methods and strategies for sticking to the difficult task of overcoming an addiction. Many people erroneously overgeneralize: they label themselves as weak and ignore the many times they were 'strong' in the face of adversity. The reality is that you can learn to persevere and work towards achieving a better life by overcoming your addictions. However, you need the proper guidance and instruction, and this book sets out to give you just that.

So, to summarize, it is our belief that the most important thing that you can do to achieve your goal of not using, say, nicotine, pills or alcohol is not to focus on all the good times and pleasure you will be giving up as a result of your change in lifestyle, but to force yourself to focus on all the benefits you will reap by making this change. The second thing is to recognize that the most important variable in being successful in giving up any addiction is to try, try and try again until you discover the right combination of activities, strategies and coping behaviours that will enable you to achieve your goal! Avoid overgeneralizing and labelling yourself a 'failure' or a 'quitter' because you have had difficulty sticking to your goal of giving up your drug of choice. Instead, recognize that you are a fallible human who, like all other humans, learns from experience and mistakes. Tell yourself that although you tried and later relapsed, each time you try again you increase the probability that this new effort at overcoming your addiction will be the time that works for the rest of your life.

Here's a practical exercise to help you begin the process of overcoming your addiction. List all the things you will gain by learning to stay free of nicotine, pills or alcohol. Here are some examples from people we have helped over the years to overcome their addictions. We will add our comments where appropriate.

'I will increase the chances that I will be able to sustain a satisfying relationship with a woman and won't destroy it by turning her off when drunk.'

'I will increase the chances of becoming more aware of what I really want and can achieve in life. Cigarettes and drink when used excessively dull my awareness.'

'I will increase the chances of experiencing the pleasure of excelling at my chosen career. Pills and alcohol do not help me to be my best at my profession.'

'I will increase the chances that people will respect me for my talents, my ability to develop my potential, and for being a good role model to others.'

'I will increase the chances of being able to live a long healthy life.' (Research shows that substances such as alcohol, cigarettes, etc., are all associated with increased likelihood of developing heart, lung and liver disease, oesophageal and stomach cancer, and early onset of strokes, all of which will either kill you or lead to a severely diminished life.) 'So by giving up cigarettes I will gain the peace of mind of knowing I am increasing the chances of remaining healthy and able to enjoy my lover, family, friends and professional success for a longer period of time!'

'I will add new friends and stop turning off potential friends and business asssociates. I will no longer have to later apologize for the stupid things I may have said or done while intoxicated.'

'I will increase the chances of having more genuine, intimate and committed relationships with the people I do keep as friends, for my true 'self' will be involved in the relationship and not some 'distorted self' which is created by the chronic use of stimulants.'

'My memory will improve, as well as other mental abilities.' (People who use drugs and alcohol reduce the ability of their brains to work effectively and efficiently. People who give up these substances realize that in time they may be able to reason abstractly with greater ease, convert their thoughts into words and express their ideas more easily and better, as well as experience an improve-ment in their short-term memory. Recovering increased mental abilities will increase your chances of achieving your other goals. A sharp mind will achieve sharp success!)

'As I stop using dope and pills I will probably feel more energetic and even motivated to stick with activities. Dope use tends to slow me down, and tends to make me more likely not to stick with something when the going gets difficult, or to throw a temper tantrum and go and lick my wounds! Success and happiness are the results of persever-ance!'

4

'I will save money and spend my money more wisely. Often, while intoxicated, I bought drinks for people who I either barely knew or cared for very little, unless of course I was drinking with them. Often, when my head was clear, I regretted having spent money impulsively while intoxicated.'

'I will have a greater chance of avoiding the dangerous situations I have found myself in while actively using drugs and alcohol.' (People under the influence of such substances are far more likely to get into verbal and physical fights, car accidents and otherwise dangerous situations, where the potential for harm to them is relatively high. People are more likely to engage in dangerous sexual practices while intoxicated, thereby greatly increasing their chances of acquiring sexually transmitted diseases like AIDS.)

'As I have grandchildren, once I have stopped living in a perpetual state of intoxication I may very well get to see and enjoy them, because my own children won't be afraid to bring them to visit me for fear I will be an unhealthy role model for them.'

'Overcoming my addictions will lead to an awareness of how to experience a more genuine joy, satisfaction and happiness.' (Addictive substances produce euphoria and feelings of relaxation, but in many ways these are rather superficial. When you give up nicotine, pills and alcohol you will have to struggle at first to discover how to create more genuine, longer-lasting feelings of calm, euphoria and relaxation. However, as you struggle with making these discoveries, the things you then do to attempt to achieve positive feelings are very likely to eventually produce very genuine, real feelings of happiness, satisfaction and even euphoria!)

Once you have completed your own list of positive reasons for overcoming your addiction, continue to add to this list and update it from time to time. Keep the list posted in your bathroom or on your refrigerator or desk where you can see it from day to day! Or simply post the following reminder:

Focus on what you are gaining and not what you are giving up!

2

Set your goal: abstinence versus controlled substance use

Why might it be better for you to make your goal abstinence rather than controlled drinking or controlled drug use? Many people who are aware that their use of, say, nicotine or alcohol has led to some problems are understandably reluctant to make total abstinence their goal. You may believe that total abstinence is unnecessary, or too hard, or would be impossible to achieve. Others may reject total abstinence because of an inability to remain mindful of all the ways that life would eventually improve if they were to successfully give up. Let us at this point consider the issue of goal-setting and whether it would be better to make your goal total abstinence or controlled intake.

Is total abstinence the best goal for all problem drinkers, smokers, or drug users? Let us first consider what research on this issue suggests is the more realistic, advantageous goal. Research on individuals with alcohol problems suggests that choosing the goal of controlled drinking versus abstinence depends largely on the characteristics of the individual drinker being considered.

For certain drinkers, controlled drinking as a goal is not a good idea; over the long run, studies show that a very large percentage of people will eventually return to heavy, regular drinking accompanied by all the problems associated with such a pattern of alcohol use. For the drinker who has been physically dependent and experienced blackouts, tremors, etc., and who is older, with a long history of problematic drinking complete with repeated failure at controlled drinking, abstinence appears to be the safer, more sensible goal. With younger drinkers who are not experiencing a high degree of symptoms of physical dependence, no medical complications, and reasonably good vocational and social functioning, moderate or controlled drinking may, and we repeat may, be a rational goal. As for other drugs, the same rule generally applies. The longer and heavier your use of the drug, the more difficult it is to use it in a controlled manner. And, of course, with some very powerful drugs like crack and heroin, controlled use is very unlikely regardless of your history with the drug. With these powerfully addictive drugs, any use is dangerous in the long run.

If at this time in your life you are not convinced that abstinence is the best goal for you and are unwilling to strive for the goal of total abstinence, then use the self-help procedures, strategies, philosophy and activities of Rational Emotive Behaviour Therapy (REBT) – which is the approach we are presenting in this book – towards the goal of controlled drinking, smoking or drug use. If after attempting controlled use you are honest with yourself and realize that abstinence is the more rational goal for you, then the methods and philosophy outlined in this book can be applied to the goal of abstinence. An important part of the philosophy of REBT is that it urges people to take responsibility for their decisions, actions and emotions and to work hard towards achieving the goals they choose for themselves. REBT encourages people to avoid illogical, 'all or nothing' reasoning, and consequently does not believe that all people must have the same goal.

Be honest with yourself and work hard towards the goal you choose. It is recommended that you do a cost-benefit analysis of the problem. List the advantages and disadvantages of your problem and of both abstinence and controlled use. If you do not believe that total abstinence is the best goal for you based on your own history then set an initial goal of moderation. Be very concrete and specify the amount of your drink or drug to be consumed, the time to be spent consuming it, and the number of times you will allow yourself to consume it per week. Accurate records have to be kept, and we recommend you clearly document a change in your pattern of usage which is maintained for a substantial period of time (at least six months) before you consider the goal of controlled use achieved. A far better strategy is to establish some self-control through a period of complete abstinence for at least six months, followed by a period of gradual experimentation with controlled us. After the period of temporary abstinence you may decide that the conservative approach is best and remain abstinent. However, you may still want to experiment with controlled use. If so, be honest with yourself and open to the feedback you can derive from observing the positive and negative consequences of your decision to return to controlled consumption. We strongly encourage you to have the courage to switch back from controlled use to total abstinence if the evidence suggests that sensible, controlled use is impossible for you. Only you can convince yourself what goal is best for you! Whatever goal you choose, work hard and follow the teachings of REBT and you will begin to achieve your underlying goal of comfort and enduring life satisfaction free from the ravages of addiction.

3

Discover the function that your addiction plays for you

An important initial step in overcoming your addictive behaviour is for you to understand the function substances such as nicotine, alcohol or tranquillizers play in your life. In all probability, your use of them serves many purposes in different situations at different times of your life. We want you to begin to see that drinking, say, or bingeing on chocolate is your way of attempting to manage the stress, unhappiness and painful emotions that all people experience when confronted with the hassles of daily living. Very often, addictive behaviour is aimed at escaping the uncomfortable feelings you have. People by their very nature are motivated to feel constantly comfortable, and alcohol, street drugs, nicotine, commonly abused prescription medications, caffeine and even food can be used to eliminate anxiety, depression, anger, shame, guilt, physical pain and other uncomfortable feelings, albeit on a temporary basis. Such substances temporarily block these painful feelings and replace them with short-lived feelings of comfort, relaxation and euphoria. They do not help you achieve these results in the long term. Indeed, you know, in your heart of hearts, the long-term havoc such things have had in your life.

You need to admit that, even though originally you may have wanted to get 'high', at this point your use of drugs and/ or alcohol helps you re-establish lost feelings of comfort. So in order to give up your use of them you will need to learn other ways of coping with or eliminating these uncomfortable feelings. This book is designed to teach you the many different skills, activities, etc., which will help you to re-establish comfortable feelings without using addictive substances. In other words, the function that drugs, alcohol, nicotine, even some foods play in your life at present will be replaced by other coping skills so that you will not need them to

11

re-establish feelings of comfort and control when encountering the difficult feelings of daily living.

Before we discuss the strategies that will help you control your use of any or all of these substances, take some time to think about the function that they have played and continue to play in your life. Do you use drugs because you experience anxiety in social situations? Do you feel anxious or depressed when you are alone and then drink or take tranquillizers? Does alcohol help you 'unwind' after a difficult day and help you to fall asleep at night? Or do chocolate or junk food help you start to do some task you find boring and are not motivated to do? Does a cigarette make you feel more comfortable with yourself?

To begin your programme of self-change, buy a small notebook which you can use to write down the function or role that these substances play in your life. Later on you can use this notebook to record other important observations relevant to your substance abuse, so that you can change your behaviour and improve your life. Your notebook can become a tool for helping you to manage your despair and anger as well as other painful emotions. But, for now, purchase the notebook and try to have it handy throughout the day. When you begin to experience the desire for, say, a cigarette or a drink, write down several things. Write down the date and the time of day you experienced the urge. Write down any external event with which your urge may be associated, such as criticism by your supervisor or an argument with your partner. If there is no clear external stressful event that is 'triggering' your craving then write down any 'internal' events, like thoughts or worries that occurred just before you experienced your urge for your preferred substance. For the purposes of this book let's call these urge triggers 'activating events' and give them the symbol 'A'. Your 'A' or 'activating event' is associated with your desire to escape discomfort by using your substance of choice. It is very important that you train yourself to become aware of the activating events that trigger your addictive desires and urges.

There are different types of activating events that trigger your craving. Some are what we refer to as 'real' activating events, some are referring to as 'imagined' activating events and some are 'internal' or 'symptom' activating events. Here are some examples of notebook entries that other people have made. Each entry will identify a different type of activating event.

Example 1 A real activating event: Jane

Journal entry date: 17/5, 4.30 p.m.
It is Friday afternoon and I feel inclined to go to happy hour to drink. The activating event is that I don't have a date for this evening and I have essentially nothing to do. I am feeling lonely and depressed.

The above activating event was real in that Jane was facing an actual situation in the here and now. Her emotional reaction to not having a date later that evening was to feel lonely and depressed.

In the next example, the activating event is an 'imagined event' because at the present time the 'dreaded' event has not occurred, but is being imagined as something that will happen in the future.

Example 2 An imagined activating event: Bob

Journal entry date: 2/9, 10.30 a.m.
I just learned of the news that my wife's routine mammogram indicated that she needs to be examined by a specialist. They said she has either a benign cyst or possibly a life-threatening tumour. We won't know which is the case until next week. I am imagining the worst and believe that she will be told she has breast cancer and she will die shortly after this diagnosis is made. I am very anxious and desperately need a drink to calm me down and to escape from my feelings.

In this example, Bob is reacting with anxiety to an imagined scenario. At the present time the reality is that Bob's wife will consult her specialist to determine exactly what her diagnosis is and whether she has breast cancer or not. However, Bob's alcohol craving is triggered by the 'imagined event' that she will receive a cancer diagnosis and die shortly thereafter. Bob reacts to this imagined scenario with anxiety and desires alcohol to calm himself down.

Another type of activating event that may trigger a craving is what we call an 'internal activating event'. In this case, a memory of an event may trigger a craving for substance use. Here is an example of a journal entry for this type of activating event.

Example 3 An internal activating event: Jim

Journal entry date: 2/10, 3.00 p.m.
It is Saturday afternoon on a boring day. I notice a craving to smoke grass like I used to in the old days on Saturday. I have a memory and the memory is an internal activating event which is triggering my current desire. I remember how I used to smoke grass in the old days and just feel so free and relaxed all afternoon long.

The last type of activating event that we want you to learn to become aware of is what we call a 'symptom activating event'. In this case an unpleasant physical symptom will be a trigger to use a drug which will relieve the symptom. Headaches, back pain, fatigue, insomnia or withdrawal sensations are all examples of symptom activating events which can trigger use of any of the addictive substances we have discussed. Here is an example of a journal entry for a symptom activating event.

Example 4 A symptom activating event: Mary

Journal entry date: 7/6, 8.15 p.m.
I have a strong desire to smoke a joint because I have a headache. I know that relaxing with hash will take away my

THE FUNCTION YOUR ADDICTION PLAYS FOR YOU

headache and I really want to smoke a joint. After that I would want to have a cup of coffee in order not to feel tired from the hash, and then I would be able to continue to push myself to do the work I have to do.

By keeping this journal and writing down the different triggers that are associated with your desire to use different substances you will become more aware of why you use them. You will discover the function that these substances have for you. Chances are that you use the same drugs for different reasons at different times of the day under different circumstances. You may use nicotine to calm down when anxious and alcohol when you are depressed. Or your choice of drugs may be marijuana, but you will accept having to drink a beer to cope with anxiety or boredom when you are unable to find someone to buy it from. Being aware of the activating events, whether they be real, imagined, internal or symptom activating events, will enable you to discover in a more sophisticated way why you use these substances. In keeping the journal you will learn the psychological issues which are associated with your addiction. With this information you can apply the coping skills that we will teach you later in this book to the specific vulnerabilities and issues you have. This new-found psychological awareness along with effort and commitment are the necessary ingredients for successfully overcoming your addiction. So buy that notebook and start keeping a journal! You may very well discover some things about yourself that will help you intelligently attack your dependency problems.

4

Realize the important role that attitudes and beliefs play in determining your emotions and self-defeating substance use

In order to overcome your addiction it is important that you recognize that your use of, say, pills or alcohol is a quick and passive way of eliminating the uncomfortable emotions that are a part of life. Drugs, alcohol, nicotine and so on quickly and effortlessly relieve the discomfort of these negative emotions which interfere with your happiness and daily life satisfaction.

The typical person generally believes that uncomfortable negative emotions like anger, depression, shame, guilt and anxiety are the inevitable consequences of experiencing some unfortunate event. For example, let us suppose that you are informed that you will be made redundant from work. This real activating event will be associated with feelings of depression, shame, anger and anxiety. The average person on the street will say that the event of losing one's job 'caused' the emotions of depression, shame, anger and anxiety. In this situation the person suffering from an addiction will often say that smoking or drinking, say, helps them feel better after losing their job and this is why they do it. But let's try and take a different look at this situation.

Instead of merely saying that drinking helps you feel better after losing your job, let us say that drinking helps you feel comfortable after becoming very uncomfortable. You are uncomfortable because you are feeling intense, painful emotions like depression, shame, anger and anxiety. The alcohol – or whatever you use – is helping you to soothe yourself by quickly eliminating or blocking you from feeling these painful emotions. The problem is that using a substance like alcohol to block off these painful feelings is at best a very temporary solution to the problem. After a few hours the painful feelings of depression, anger, shame and anxiety are experienced once again as the body metabolizes the alcohol. At this point you may choose to take some more alcohol into your system to soothe yourself again, but – alas – the relief will again be temporary.

There is a different way of coping with the unpleasant feelings of depression, anger, shame and anxiety associated with the real activating event of losing your job. Instead of seeing these intense emotions as being solely caused by the unfortunate event of losing your job, you can acknowledge that your beliefs about this event influence the feelings you experience in response to it. Let us put this episode into the ABC framework that REBT is famous for. In this episode, 'A' is the real activating event, 'B' stands for the beliefs about this event, and 'C' stands for the consequences of A × B.

A Real activating event: You learn that your employer is laying you off from work.

B Beliefs:
1 Poor me! It is unfair that I was laid off when others at the company still have their jobs. This unfair event absolutely should not or must not happen to me!
2 It is awful and terrible that this has happened to me.
3 I cannot stand being out of work and having to push myself to find another job.
4 Losing my job proves I am inadequate compared to everyone else. I am a real loser.
5 Other people will think less of me for having lost my job. I must have them think well of me. I need their approval.
6 I must have a drink and get high. I need relief from the uncomfortable feelings and worries I have. I cannot stand the pain and the frustration of losing my job.

C Emotional and behavioural consequences of **A** × **B**:
1 I feel anxious, depressed, shameful and angry.

2 I go out and get drunk to soothe my uncomfortable feelings.

The point we are making here is that emotional reactions are controlled by the beliefs you have about the unfortunate things that happen to you. They are *not* caused by the events themselves. Appreciating and accepting this idea is crucial because it will help you in reducing the strong and unpleasant feelings that encourage you to use, say, tranquillizers or drugs to restore your comfort level.

To further convince you of this important point, consider the following scenario. Imagine that one hundred people lose their jobs. Imagine further that all of these one hundred people are of equal intelligence and all have families that rely on their income. Also, suppose that all of these people are of the same experience level and educational level, so that the degree of difficulty of finding another job would be the same for all one hundred individuals. And last, imagine that they all enjoyed the nature of their work, their supervisor and colleagues at the job to the same degree. The question we want you to consider is this: Would all one hundred individuals who had lost their jobs experience the same degree of emotional upset, or would they experience different feelins at varying intensity? If you think carefully about this question, you will acknowledge that the emotional reaction these one hundred people had to the same problematic event would differ. Some would feel suicidal over the loss of their jobs, while some would feel sad, some would be displeased and others would feel annoyed. The explanation for the difference in emotional reactions would be due to each person's beliefs about the meaning of the job loss and about the discomfort they would encounter in attempting to obtain another satisfying job. Those people who thought that they cold not stand the inconveniences and steps necessary for obtaining another job would be far more disturbed about it than those who acknowledged that they would experience discomfort, but believed they could tolerate this discomfort and that it would be worth tolerating it.

You will move closer to overcoming your addiction if you change how you think about your emotional reactions to life's difficult events. Begin to recognize that problems, obstacles and injustices that you encounter give you an opportunity to get upset, but that you cause yourself to get upset. Rather than seeing yourself as the victim of your strong emotional reactions to life events that are caused by the unfortunate things that happen to you, start seeing yourself as being responsible for your self-defeating emotions.

To better appreciate the primary role your beliefs play in determining your emotional upset, consider this example from the sport of fishing. The activating events of life – that is, the problems and obstacles of life – are to you what bait is to a fish. Some fish take the bait hook, line and sinker! Likewise, by learning the methods and philosophy of Rational Emotive Behaviour Therapy you will empower yourself to avoid taking the bait and getting yourself self-destructively upset when people do malicious things to you or life presents you with difficult challenges and obstacles. Also, the method of this approach will help you to control the damage once you become upset or hooked. This approach will help you calm yourself down and bring your behaviour under self-control without having to resort to the soothing effects of addictive substances. This self-help approach will enable you to re-establish the equilibrium you lost when you made yourself upset! Making this shift will empower you and start you on the road to overcoming your addiction and to liberating yourself from the costs of being addicted.

Many people will reject the idea that they are primarily responsible for their self-defeating feelings when things go wrong in their life. This is because people, by nature, dislike hard work and find working at emotional self-control to be uncomfortable. By acknowledging the role you play in creating the disturbed emotions that lead to your addictive behaviour you then become responsible for your actions and your addiction. Many people would prefer to blame external factors rather than take responsibility for their feelings and behaviour.

Unfortunately, many people stay addicted because of their unwillingness to change how they think about things. Rather, they will blame their parents, their environment, their lack of job and opportunities, or see their self-defeating behaviour as stemming from a disease they are powerless to control.

The emphasis being made here is that, regardless of what happens to you, how you think about things largely determines how you feel and how you behave. This straightforward idea is simple to understand, but difficult to put into practice. Rather than depress yourself by thinking, 'it is too hard to learn to think differently so I don't have to rely on drink (or pills, or cigarettes) to reduce my uncomfortable feelings,' try adopting a different perspective. Recognize that although you will experience some difficulty in learning to think differently, there is no reason to believe that you will not be able to tolerate this difficulty, and that as you do so, changing your beliefs will get easier and easier the more practice you put in. Recognize that, like nearly everything in life, the more you practise something the better you get at doing it. Most of you who smoke hash had to learn to roll a joint. You learned how to roll the joint because you did not let the initial difficulty you encountered stop you from practising how to roll a smooth marijuana joint. Likewise you could also learn to think differently, so that when things go wrong you do not get so upset that you have to turn to, say, binge eating to restore your comfort. Although it may be difficult, if you remember to focus on and always keep in mind how your life will slowly improve when you stop relying on your addictive substances (see Chapter 1), you will continue to practise thinking differently so that you become free of your addiction!

In the next chapter, we will help you to distinguish between rational and irrational beliefs.

5

Appreciate the difference between rational and irrational beliefs

In the last chapter, we introduced the idea that it is your beliefs about what happens to you that primarily create your disturbed feelings of anxiety, depression, shame, anger, guilt and self-pity. The idea is probably the most important single concept of this book, for if you learn to use this idea you will be empowered by it! Life, the world and others can often be difficult, unfair, etc., but these things do not cause you to feel terribly upset. Recognizing that it is what you tell yourself about the difficulties and obstacles you face is what really determines how upset you get and whether you then turn to an addiction for relief from your self-created misery. As we said in the last chapter, life tosses us the bait, but we have a choice as to whether we bite on the bait and swallow it hook, line and sinker, or whether we avoid taking it! The methods and beliefs taught in this book will not only show you how to avoid biting on the bait and upsetting yourself, but also show you how to 'unhook' yourself, and restore your equilibrium. Drink and the like may numb your pain, and do so fairly quickly, but they won't help you to deal with life's hassles in a healthy manner.

As we have said, the approach to self-change we are using in this book is called Rational Emotive Behaviour Therapy (REBT). It was developed by a famous American clinical psychologist called Dr Albert Ellis, who has taught thousands of people that the primary reason they get upset when things go wrong is because they hold a set of irrational beliefs about life's adversities. There are four types of irrational beliefs:

- demanding beliefs (where you demand that you must get what you want and must not get what you don't want);
- awfulizing beliefs (where you take life's adversities and turn them into horrors);

23

- low discomfort tolerance (LDT) beliefs (where you think that you cannot tolerate what is difficult to tolerate);
- depreciation beliefs (where you put down or devalue yourself, other people and/or life conditions).

Let us list several general irrational beliefs people have that create disturbed emotions which are then soothed by, say, drugs, cigarettes and alcohol:

1 Life must be easy and smooth and problems absolutely should not occur.
2 When a problem occurs I really can't stand the discomfort of facing it without the soothing effects of a cigarette.
3 I absolutely need a quick and easy way out of my problems.
4 I have to have the things I want because I deserve them! It's awful when I don't get what I deserve.
5 People must be the way I want them to be. People must be nice, fair, honest, loyal, kind, warm, etc., and when they are not, it's awful.
6 My addiction problem makes me less worthwhile or less adequate than people who do not have an addiction problem and are able to achieve more in life.

These are just six examples of the many irrational beliefs that create emotional disturbance which you relieve with, say, drink or tranquillizers. Each one of these beliefs may at first appear 'normal' to you in the sense that many people in our society would agree to them. However, it can be shown they are invalid, untrue, illogical, inconsistent with reality much of the time, self-defeating, and therefore irrational!

The irrational beliefs that create emotional upset are self-defeating because they interfere with your ability to adapt to and cope with the numerous challenges and problems that you encounter in life. Rational beliefs (which we will consider later) help you respond to the obstacles and problems of life in such a way that you do not harm yourself and that you make the best of a bad situation. Rational beliefs are scientifically valid, which means they are consistent with external reality and they make sense or are logical. Because rational beliefs are consistent with reality you can gather evidence to show they are true and not just ideas you subjectively believe are true! Rational beliefs are self-enhancing: that is, they help you adapt and cope when the going gets rough, and instead of jeopardizing your future well-being they help to preserve it. Let us take a closer look at the six irrational beliefs that we have just mentioned and see how they differ from rational beliefs.

Irrational Belief 1: Life must be easy and smooth and problems absolutely should not occur

This is irrational because it is a demand as to how life absolutely should or must be! It is irrational because there is no evidence that supports the idea that, because you and many other people believe that life absolutely should or must be easy, it therefore follows that it will be that way. Unfortunately, humans forget that they do not have the power of gods and cannot dictate the way things 'must' be. A rational belief that would be a reasonable substitute for this one is 'I would really like or prefer that life be easy and smooth and be free of problems, but unfortunately it does not have to be that way! If I were a god, I could create a universe where there were no problems, but unfortunately I am not that powerful. I can attempt to resolve my problems with my available talents so that my life is a bit easier. Demanding that life must be the way I want it to be will lead to emotional disturbance that will create a strong desire for drugs or alcohol. Preferring life to be easy without the demand allows me to roll with the punches of life without misusing my preferred substances.'

Irrational Belief 2: When a problem occurs I really can't stand the discomfort of facing it without the soothing effects of something to help

This irrational belief and others similar to it are the reason you have what is called low discomfort tolerance. It is irrational because there is actually no evidence that you really cannot stand or tolerate the discomfort created by the problem you have encountered. There is a great deal of evidence that you strongly dislike the problem and the discomfort you are experiencing. There is much evidence that you would be more comfortable if you were not facing the problem. The discomfort caused by this and other problems at best makes it difficult or even very difficult for you to stand or tolerate facing the problem without the soothing effects of drugs, say, or comfort eating. However, although you may dislike the discomfort it is wrong to conclulde that you cannot stand it. When you tell yourself, 'I can't stand these uncomfortable feelings, I must have or need the soothing effects of hash or chocolate,' you actually lower your discomfort tolerance! In order to overcome your dependence it is important for you to raise your discomfort tolerance by changing your beliefs about your obstacles and the discomfort you experience. A rational belief you could use would be, 'When a problem occurs, while I dislike the discomfort I experience, I really can tolerate these uncomfortable feelings. The discomfort caused by my problem fuels my effort to deal with it and remedy it. Although a smoke (say) would temporarily soothe these feelings, there are several good reasons not to escape this discomfort. My preferred substance will impair my judgement and behaviour, making me much less likely to deal with the problem effectively. It can make me numb so that I lose my motivation to deal with the problem, and this is very likely to allow the problem to worsen with time. Addictive substances are unhealthy, both physically and psychologically, in the sense that they weaken my discomfort tolerance and make me less and less able to function well!'

Irrational Belief 3: I absolutely need a quick and easy way out of my problems

This belief is irrational because there is no evidence that can be gathered to prove it is true! To prove to yourself it is untrue that you absolutely need a quick and easy way out of your problems, consider what happens when you don't find a quick and easy way out. The worst that happens is that some unfortunate consequence happens and you experience discomfort because you dislike the consequence. People set themselves up to use drugs, alcohol, tranquillizers, nicotine and so on because these substances offer a quick and easy way out of problems and the associated discomfort in the short run! However, in the long run the problem is still there and continues to worsen. You would be better able to resist using these things if you said to yourself, 'Although I want a quick and easy way out of this problem, I really don't absolutely need one. A quick and easy solution would only restore my comfort sooner, but I really can tolerate discomfort as I slowly find my way out of any problems even if I strongly dislike the slow path to comfort! Going for the quick fix will only add to my addiction.'

Irrational Belief 4: I have to have the things I want because I deserve them! It's awful when I don't get what I deserve

This belief is self-defeating, because when you don't get what you think you deserve and you believe that this is awful you experience a depression that is based on self-pity. Unfortunately, while there may be some relationship between what we get and what we deserve, frequently there is no connection between the two. The universe and life are often cruel and unfair and do not have the same rules of deservingness as we do! This mismatch between what we think we deserve and what the universe gives us leads to self-pity when we demand that life is fair to us, and these feelings of self-pity set you up to turn to addictive substances to soothe your emotional pain. Of course, since you cannot change the universe, the way out of this self-created emotional trap is to give up your demands for fairness. Accept that life is often unfair, cruel, difficult and full of hassles, and that, no matter how much you complain that you deserve better treatment, it doesn't follow that you must get such fairer treatment. Your demand will not change reality and magically create what you deserve. Rather, it will only create emotional disturbances. Instead, harness your feelings of displeasure and disappointment which are appropriate when you don't get what you want and use them to fuel your efforts to work towards solving your problems and reaching your goals. If you change your demand for fairness to acceptance of reality then you will still want to get what you think you deserve, and you may decide to strive for it, but you will know when to give up and you will experience dissappointment and displeasure if you don't get what you deserve. These feelings are good, in the sense that they fuel your motivation to try to change what you dislike and to adapt when you can't change it. Thus, by giving up your demand that you must get what you subjectively believe you deserve, you will not change the healthy feelings of disappointment and displeasure into self-pity and anger, which are less healthy and may well lead you back to the costly and temporary relief that addictive substances will bring.

Irrational Belief 5: People must be the way I want them to be. People must be nice, fair, honest, loyal, kind, warm, etc., and when they are not, it's awful

This belief is irrational for many different reasons. Let's look at the practical disadvantage it creates. We all know that our fellow humans are not always nice, fair, honest, loyal, kind, warm, etc., and neither are you! By holding on to the belief that they *must* be kind and loyal, etc., you are setting yourself up to experience strong emotional reactions of anger, rage, hurt and depression which will fuel your desire to escape your self-created emotional misery through the temporary relief of, say, drugs, nicotine and alcohol. So the practical advantage of modifying this belief would be to experience the healthier but more realistic feelings of annoyance, displeasure and disappointment when people act the way you dislike. Consider adopting the following rational belief: 'Although I badly want people to be nice, fair, honest, loyal, kind, warm, etc., they don't have to be this way. They usually act the way they want and not the way I want. This is very unfortunate, but hardly awful. Demanding that they act in the way I want them to sets me up to get intensely disturbed. I don't run the universe and although I want people to be a certain way I do not have the power to move mountains! I can try to influence them by persuasion or reinforcing the kinds of actions I strongly prefer. These attempts will increase the chances that they will act the way I want but never guarantee it! Tough! This is the way it is! Now I can either disturb myself with my demands or change my beliefs to preferences and accept that not all my preferences will be met!'

Irrational Belief 6: My addiction problem makes me less worthwhile or less adequate than people who do not have such a problem and are able to achieve more in life

There are several practical advantages for giving up this belief. Thinking about people as rateable entities with more or less worth leads to self-defeating feelings of shame, guilt, depression and anger directed towards yourself. These feelings are self-defeating because they do not help you find the hope and motivation to overcome your strong habit called addiction. Instead, this self-depreciation point of view contributes to hopelessness, despair and helplessness, all of which will set you up to turn to your addiction to soothe your self-hate!

Obviously there are many reasons why it would be far better if you did not have, or soon overcame, your addiction problem. Some of these reasons include greater productivity which increases satisfaction and benefits both you and others, longer-lasting feelings of pleasure and achievement, greater stability of mood, greater tolerance, patience and sensitivity shown to others, etc. However, although it is far better for you to improve your functioning by giving up alcohol or drugs it does not follow that your worth goes up if you do or goes down if you don't. If you think of your worth as a person as constant then you will not be vulnerable to hating yourself if you relapse in the future. Your behaviour can be rated, and it is better if you live healthily than living with your addiction, but just because it is better it doesn't follow that you are better if you do so. As we shall show you later in this book, unconditional self-acceptance is the healthy alternative to conditional self-esteem, so work towards giving up your addiction and accept yourself along the way.

By encouraging yourself to give up the absolute 'shoulds' or 'musts' that you use to define your conditional self-worth and to develop unconditional self-acceptance instead, you will derive many benefits. First, you will still feel negative feelings because you will rate your behaviour and the consequences which follow from it. So by rating your habit of avoiding discomfort through your addiction as a bad or self-defeating habit, you will begin to feel appropriately regretful when you consider the negative consequences that have come from this habit and will likely come in the future. The concern for your health and the displeasure and disappointment associated with not developing your potential and getting into other hassles and problems will help you to feel deeply motivated to break this habit and develop alternative habits which are healthier and more self-enhancing. By developing unconditional self-acceptance you will not create the hopelessness that goes with believing you are inadequate and worthless. These feelings will not help you push yourself to give up the habit! And since you are a fallible human prone to error, with unconditional self-acceptance you will have fewer problems with relapses. As we said earlier, if you relapse, which is likely because it takes most people multiple efforts to become more skilled at living without their addiction, you will not fall into a deep depression and hopeless pit of self-pity when you are struggling to get better and better at thinking rationally and living without alcohol, or cigarettes, or drugs!

Conclusion

The way to overcome your addiction problem is to learn to identify the irrational beliefs you hold that make you disturb yourself when things do not go the way you would like. Once you learn to identify the specific beliefs that are creating your self-defeating feelings of anger, depression, self-pity, shame, guilt and anxiety, you can begin to think about how you might change what you believe so that you do not disturb yourself when things go wrong. If you learn to modify your irrational beliefs so that you develop more rational beliefs and learn to think more rationally more of the time, you will still experience negative feelings when you encounter problems, hassles and obstacles. It is important that you note that feelings of regret, concern, disappointment, displeasure, annoyance and sadness are very appropriate reactions that help motivate you to change whatever it is that you dislike. They fuel your effort to respond with helpful behaviour to the problems you encounter from the external world. Whether you feel mildly disappointed or strongly disappointed, you will still be more in control of yourself than if you experience feelings of anger and depression. The point is that if you encounter an obstacle and have rational beliefs you will still have negative feelings, but these negative feelings won't be the kind that lead you to resort to your addiction to relieve them. Learning not to disturb yourself so that you can stop resorting to your addiction takes work and practice! Again, ask yourself how badly you want all the positive consequences that will sooner or later come if you give up your strong habit. It is important that you realize that if you have an addiction then you probably have a low discomfort tolerance, and that for years you have drunk, taken drugs, smoked or binged to soothe yourself at the slightest bit of discomfort! Your addiction is really a strong habit – for that is what addiction really means, a strong habit of reducing any sort of displeasure or discomfort quickly and passively by taking a substance that alters the chemicals in your brain. In order to overcome this strong habit you will have to practise thinking differently so that you do not disturb yourself. However, even if you learn to develop rational beliefs to replace your other irrational beliefs, you will still feel negative emotions like sadness, concern, disappointment and annoyance which will require you to have a reasonably high level of discomfort tolerance! Nevertheless, these healthier emotional reactions will make it more likely that you will tackle your problems without resorting to addictive substances.

In the next chapter, we will build on what we have discussed so far about irrational beliefs and show you how you can identify and dispute them forcefully.

6

Identify and forcefully dispute your self-defeating irrational beliefs

Now that we have discussed the role of irrational thinking in creating the low discomfort tolerance that leads to addiction, it is important to address ways of changing your irrational thinking. In the last chapter it was shown how irrational thinking is reflected in dogmatic commands and demands, awfulizing beliefs, low discomfort tolerance beliefs and depreciation beliefs. Rational beliefs are more flexible and non-extreme and are reflected in preferences, anti-awfulizing beliefs, high discomfort tolerance beliefs and acceptance beliefs. When you are emotionally disturbed or experiencing the discomfort of coming down from your high you automatically seek to escape the discomfort you erroneously believe you 'can't stand'. It is important that you learn to use the technique of disputing during moments of discomfort in order to gain control over your automatic, habitual response to escape discomfort through using more drugs, alcohol, tranquillizers, etc.

Disputing is the process whereby you attempt to change your thinking so that you begin to think more rationally and take control of your behaviour. Dispute is a thinking process, and like any other human activity at first it will be awkward and uncomfortable and you will probably not do it very well. But just as you practised using your drugs and developed skill at rolling joints, mixing drinks, borrowing money and hiding chocolate, if you really want to you can practise disputing and become very good at it. The reward will be that you will develop more adaptive, self-enhancing beliefs that will prevent you from disturbing yourself and enable you to develop greater self-control over your self-defeating impulsive behaviour. The more you sincerely practise disputing, the more you will learn to replace self-defeating behaviour with intelligent behaviour, which will ultimately help you to live a productive addiction-free lifestyle.

To begin to learn to dispute your irrational beliefs, you need first to identify them. Here are some questions you can ask yourself to help you to identify your irrational beliefs.

- 'What am I telling myself or believing that is making me so upset?'
- 'What am I telling myself that is leading me to want to take drugs, smoke, binge or drink?'
- 'What am I telling myself that is making me so upset that I am willing to throw away tomorrow in exchange for escaping the discomfort of the present?'
- 'How am I making myself upset? What am I demanding of others, the world, life, or even myself?'
- 'What is the "must" or "should" that I am saying to myself that is getting me so upset?'
- 'What is the "have to" or "need" that I am fooling myself into believing that is making my discomfort so high and my tolerance for standing it so low?'
- 'How am I making myself angry, depressed discouraged, anxious, fearful, ashamed, guilty, jealous or hurt?'
- 'Am I telling myself that what I am facing is awful or the end of the world?'
- 'Am I telling myself that I can't stand the situation and/or the feelings I have about the situation?'
- 'Am I putting myself down in this situation?'
- 'Am I putting others down in this situation?'

The next set of questions can be used to motivate yourself to challenge your irrational beliefs once you have found them.

- 'Would I not be better off and empowered by assuming responsibility for my beliefs and the self-defeating feelings and behaviours they lead to rather than making myself weak and powerless by believing that I can't learn to control my beliefs, feelings and behaviour?'

- 'Although it may be very difficult at first, why can't I learn to dispute my beliefs and take control of my emotional reactions and behavioural reactions to the obstacles of life?'
- 'Why can't I learn to think differently than my parents did? Why can't I give up the self-defeating beliefs they taught me?'
- 'Why can't I learn to push myself to learn to dispute and think more rationally?'
- 'If at first learning to think differently and learning to cope with obstacles differently is difficult, why can't I push myself to do what is difficult so that I can achieve the rewards my effort will bring?'
- 'How badly do I want to overcome my tendency of depending on this addiction instead of learning to rely on my own acquired strengths to cope with problems and get what I want?'
- 'What will I gain in the present and in the future if I work and practise at disputing and learning to tolerate discomfort without soothing myself with my addiction?'
- 'Why must it be easy to change a strong habit? Why can't I strongly practise changing a strong habit even if I wish the process were easier?'
- 'Where is the evidence that I cannot try, try, try again until I learn all the steps necessary for overcoming my strong habit?'
- 'Am I really too tired to continue trying to change or am I really creating my own self-pity by believing it should be easier to change than it is? Although I may be tired, why can't I continue working at this self-change process? Remember, I used to continue to party when I was tired, so if I really want to I can continue with this process!'
- 'Why not choose to learn to give up this habit because it has already produced so much pain and suffering in me? Do I really want to choose more losses and more suffering?'
- 'Is it not a safe assumption that the more I practise these skills the easier they will get and the less discomfort I will feel? Isn't the investment in time and energy worth the

pleasures and rewards I will ultimately get? Do I have the pleasures and rewards firmly in mind so I can use them to motivate me to stand the discomfort?'

Now here are some illustrative questions to help you to challenge your irrational beliefs once you have pin-pointed them.

- 'Why *must* I have the love and approval of others? Is it not really true that I want the love and approval of certain people, but I can exist quite well without it?'
- 'Do I really need the love and approval of certain significant people in order to accept myself? Why can't I choose to accept myself unconditionally even if others reject me as inadequate? Does what they believe matter more than what I believe?'
- 'Does life *have to* be smooth and easy and fair the way I am demanding it to be? Since I do not run the universe would I not be better off if I gave up my childish belief that life has to be the way I want it to be?'
- 'Just because I have, say, used alcohol for years, how does that prove I am powerless over my habit? Habits are made through practice, so why can't I push myself to develop healthy habits for coping with my cravings until they pass?'

Disputing involves asking yourself questions and pushing yourself to answer them logically so that you develop adaptive beliefs and learn to bring your feelings and behaviours under control. Disputing involves attempting to think about the evidence that really exists for endorsing one belief over another. Disputing involves thinking scientifically and testing your beliefs to determine which are true and which are exaggerated, false beliefs that are not helpful in coping with life. Disputing is a skill like reading, riding a bicycle or learning to swim. Everyone is capable of becoming good at disputing their irrational beliefs, but practice is the only way of getting good at this skill.

The next step is for you to answer the disputing question you have asked yourself. As you do so, try and develop really persuasive answers to your questions. The more you really believe your rational beliefs, the more you will help yourself in the long run. Here are some persuasive answers to the above disputing questions.

- I don't have to have the love and approval of others, although it would be very nice if they did approve of me. I can, of course, exist quite well when others don't approve of me, but I could exist better if they do.
- I can accept myself even when significant others don't show me love and approval. My worth is constant and does not go up and down according to whether I'm loved or not. If they reject me because I have some unfortunate habits, like being addicted to drink, then I can still accept myself with my addiction and work steadily to overcome it.
- No, life doesn't have to be smooth and easy, although I would like it to be. I can definitely tolerate it when I get hassle in my life and don't need to drug or intoxicate myself if I am hassled. Tolerating hassle leads me to deal better with it. Demanding an easy life will mean living an addicted life.
- I am not powerless over my addiction and can kick the habit if I practise thinking straight. I have power over my brain, which works much better when addiction free.

In the next chapter we will show you how to think rationally in the face of temptation.

7

Cope with temptation by thinking rationally to stay in control

Let us take a look at how disputing can be useful to helping to develop the ability to stay away from bars, pubs or other high-risk situations in which you will be tempted to abandon your commitment to overcome your dependency. In analysing a typical temptation scenario we will help you to identify and dispute the irrational beliefs that lead to anger, anxiety, depression and other forms of emotional disturbance. If you are to overcome your strong habit of addiction you will have to learn to control your emotional reactions when you are in these types of difficult, tempting situations.

Scenario

You decide to try and stay away from bars and engage in other activities instead of drinking on a Friday night. When Friday evening arrives you feel lonely and depressed and severely tempted to go and have a drink. So you ask yourself, 'What am I telling myself to make me so lonely and depressed?' and 'What am I telling myself to tempt me to be so strongly tempted to go to a bar?' Possible irrational beliefs you come up with in answer to this question could be:

1 I *cannot stand* missing out on the good times I would be having at the bar.
2 I *must* have a drink to make me feel less depressed.
3 Poor me! I *must* be able to drink like everyone else.
4 I *deserve* a reward after working all week. I have to have just one drink!
5 It is *too hard* to go to the cinema or go out with a new acquaintance who does not go drinking on Friday evenings. Doing this is not fun and I *need* fun and excitement!

6 I *need* to be with my old friends. I *can't stand* excluding myself from all my addicted friends and the good times!

7 How will I ever meet someone to have a relationship with if I can't go to bars? I am lonely and I really *need* a relationship so I *must* go to the bar in order to find someone to love.

Unless you learn to change your beliefs in this type of situation you will not start the journey towards a better life. This situation is applicable whether you are a Sunday afternoon beer-drinker who watches football with your friends or someone who does drugs all alone in the mornings. As soon as you try to live without your addiction there will be times when you think back to what you would normally be doing at a certain time and who you would be drinking or doing drugs with. Unless you can change your beliefs about making new acquaintances and finding new ways to spend and enjoy your free time you will go straight back to your addiction right after committing yourself once again to give it up.

So, to begin to dispute the above irrational beliefs, left us take each separately and try to see why they are false and how to change them so that you can begin to think more rationally about the situation and your dilemma. Remember, the first step in changing your behaviour to get control over your life is to change how you think about things. So push yourself to carefully read and understand the way the following irrational beliefs are disputed and how a more rational perspective emerges from this process of questioning.

To dispute Irrational Belief 1: 'I *can't stand* missing out on the good times I would be having at the bar', ask yourself the following questions:

• Why can't I stand not going to the bar?
• Is it that I can stand missing out on the fun but would rather not have to make this sacrifice in order to achieve my long-term goal?

- Is it difficult to stand avoiding the bar, or is it impossible to stand avoiding the bar?
- Where is the evidence that I will die if I don't go to the bar?
- Is there not evidence that I actually can stand not going to the bar but that it is difficult, especially because I am not used to spending my free time doing other things besides drinking?

Answering these questions will help to develop the following rational philosophy: 'It is possible for me to tolerate not going to the bar. Yes, it may be difficult, but there is no reason why I can't do what is difficult! Certainly at first it will be a challenge to find other ways of enjoying myself without drinking, but if I keep searching I will discover how to enjoy myself in new ways. Most activities require me to develop a taste for the particular type of enjoyment that the new activity will provide. So I will push myself to go out with different people and do different things to help distract myself from returning to drink. It won't kill me to try new sports, activities, hobbies and friends. I really can stand the discomfort of trying new things even if I dislike having to experiment with new ways of spending my free time.'

To dispute Irrational Belief 2: 'I *must* have a drink to make me feel less depressed', ask yourself the following questions:

- Why *must* I have a drink to feel less depressed?
- Why do I *have to* escape this feeling of depression through drinking?
- Why can't I search for the irrational demands that are creating my depression to relieve me of it?
- Why can't I search for healthier activities like taking a walk, going to the movies, going window-shopping, riding a bicycle, going to the gym, taking a bath or having a nice meal, or calling a non-addicted friend in order to help me get through this evening when I am feeling down?
- Am I creating my depression by demanding that my life be

41

easy and the way I want it to be, like a child who cries incessantly for the things it wants?

- Am I telling myself 'Poor me, I don't *deserve* to have to work to find new ways of enjoying my free time'?
- What are the specific demands, 'musts', or 'I can't stand its' that I am using to make myself feel depressed?

Answering these questions will again help to make you think rationally along these lines: 'It is quite possible for me to tolerate depression without having to escape into my addiction. Disputing my irrational beliefs will help me to overcome my feelings of depression and to deal with the problems that I am facing. I don't have to have a drink although I want one very badly. I do not have to immediately escape the painful feeling of depression. I can tolerate this pain at least long enough to identify the irrational beliefs that are underpinning it so that I can change them. Changing the irrational beliefs that lead to my depression is a better solution than drinking to escape the depression.'

If you are making yourself depressed by silently complaining to yourself and demanding that your life must be easy, acknowledge this self-defeating habit! Push yourself to stop demanding that life be easy and the way you want it to be! Stop silently complaining to yourself, because that only makes your depression worse. Instead, accept that life is often difficult even if you and the rest of the human race wish it were always blissful. Encourage yourself to give up your belief that you should not have to work so hard to find new ways of enjoying life. Encourage yourself to accept however much work is involved in making a better life for yourself free of addiction. It is only by giving up your preconceived notions of how much work absolutely should be involved in changing and by also being willing to do whatever it takes to achieve your goal that you will be successful. Re-read and think about this rational perspective until you internalize it. Write all or part of it on a small index card, put it in your pocket and consult it several times a day. This will help you to think about what it takes to achieve your goal when the going gets rough! The first step in learning to believe a more rational, helpful perspective is to at least be familiar with the rational argument. The more you say it over and over to yourself, the more you will come to believe it. As a child, you at first imitated your parents and the things they said. After doing this many times you eventually came to develop beliefs through the process of imitation and modelling.

To dispute Irrational Belief 3: 'Poor me! I must be able to drink like everyone else', ask the following questions:

- Why do I have to be able to drink like everyone else?
- Why must life be fair and allow me to be like everyone else?
- How does my self-pity, which comes from demanding that I have what I want, help me achieve my long-term goals?
- What is a more rational and helpful perspective I could have about choosing to be different and give up my addiction?

Answering these questions will lead to you adopting the following rational philosophy: 'I do not have to have the pleasures that others experience with alcohol. I may want these pleasures, but I don't have to have them! Everything has its price, and the price of having a better life is giving up the short-lived pleasures of alcohol. Even if there are some people who can drink moderately I am, unfortunately, not one of them and I can accept this grim reality without putting myself down or silently complaining about it.'

To dispute Irrational Belief 4: 'I *deserve* a reward after working all week. I *have to* have just one drink!', ask yourself the following questions:

- Do I have to have a special reward for working all week above the salary I receive?
- Does the reward have to be a drink?
- Why do I have to have one drink?

43

- What are the other things I can give myself as a reward which will not pose a threat to my long-term well-being?

Answering these questions will help you to think along the following rational lines: 'Demanding special rewards for tolerating the discomfort of working is self-defeating for me. First of all, many people work and put up with all sorts of hassles without having to give themselves "special" rewards for doing so. I get paid for my job! That is my reward. I set myself up for self-pity by believing that I deserve an additional special reward and that I have to have what I deserve. If I want to give myself a reward, I can choose things that won't hurt me in the long run! I badly want a drink, but I don't have to have one! I won't die without drinking, but I may die if I drink! Although I badly want a drink, I am choosing to tolerate the discomfort of not giving in to this urge. I can stand this discomfort until it passes and my future will be far better in so many ways if I stick to the task. I can find something else to occupy my mind and give me some other kind of healthy pleasure! I can treat myself to a film, a dinner or something that does not cost anything, like a walk or a bike ride in the park.'

There is a saying that one drink is too many and a thousand is not enough! Having that first drink is going to set you up to continue drinking all night long. It is easier to tolerate the discomfort of avoiding the initial drink than the discomfort of stopping after the first drink. Be conservative and realistic here. Alcohol, nicotine, drugs and the like lower your discomfort tolerance and distort and impair your ability to judge what is best for you. Why not be conservative and avoid the first drink altogether rather than trick yourself into believing that maybe you will be able to stop after one drink? Why not err on the side of abstinence, at least for the first six months, before you try to see if you can learn to drink reasonably? Tell yourself you will decide whether to allow yourself to have one drink after six months of abstinence. You can stand giving up drinking for this period! This short-term approach may help you when you are very tempted. In six months, you hopefully will recognize that it just is not worth it to start trying to use addictive substances because you really don't need them and your life is so much better without them.

To dispute Irrational Belief 5: 'It is *too hard* to go to the cinema or go out with a new acquaintance who does not go drinking on Friday evenings. Doing this is not fun and I *need* fun and excitement!', ask yourself the following questions:

- Is it really *too hard* to go to the cinema or make a new friend who has a more balanced life and does not have to go drinking every Friday night in order to have a good time?
- Or is it just a challenge to find a couple of new friends who I can really enjoy hanging out with but who don't have to be drinking or drugging in order to have lots of laughs and fun?
- How do I know that I can't have fun without a drink?
- How do I know that over time I might not learn to deeply enjoy the stimulating conversation and intimate self-disclosure that goes with having a clear head?
- Do I *need* fun and excitement or do I just want it?
- Why can't I obtain the fun and excitement I crave in some other ways through other activities rather than just counting on alcohol and bars to give me this outlet?

Answering these questions will help you to develop these rational beliefs: 'Although it is initially a challenge to find new people and new activities to occupy my weekends and free time, with effort I can meet this challenge. Yes, at first it may be difficult to learn to enjoy myself on a Friday evening without getting drunk, but there is no evidence that it is unbearably difficult. I really can stand the discomfort of trying new activities until I develop an appetite for them. Being addicted requires me to actively pursue pleasure. Addictive chemicals like drugs, alcohol and nicotine produce pleasurable feelings while I passively enjoy them. So at first I will have to pursue activities in a more *active* way in order to experience pleasure. But just as I kept going to the pub, if I keep going to the gym, the cinema, the coffee house, the museum, the church or the library, I will sooner or later learn to look forward to the free time I spend there. I will experience the excitement or social stimulation I want in some of these places, or I will exchange the excitement I once had on Friday nights for the fun, excitement, social stimulation and other benefits that come from doing new activities. I can push myself to experiment doing different things with different people until I discover new and healthier ways of passing my free time. I really *can stand the discomfort* of engaging in this type of experiment. I will keep in focus all that I will gain to help me to stick with this process!'

To dispute Irrational Belief 6: 'I *need* to be with my old friends. I *can't stand* excluding myself from all my addicted friends and the good times!', ask yourself the following questions:

- Where is the evidence that I need to be with my old friends?
- Where is the evidence that I can't stand excluding myself from all my addicted friends and the good times?
- Is it not closer to the truth to say that I want to be with my old addicted friends and experience the good times, but I really can stand not to go out with them because of the negative consequences of drinking?
- If my friends are really my friends, why can't I see them in other places where drinking is not part of the activity?
- If my friends are unwilling or do not make the time to do other things with me besides drinking, what does that say about their dependency on alcohol and their desire for my friendship and companionship?
- What will I gain if I tolerate the discomfort of excluding myself from the bar scene?
- How badly do I want to avoid the problems, health consequences, etc., that go with drinking?

Again, answering these questions will help you to adopt the

46

following rational ideas: 'I do have the internal strength to become more self-reliant and less dependent on my addicted friends. It is fine to want to be with my friends, but since I don't need to be with them I refuse to endanger my health and future by drinking with them. At first it will be difficult, but I can live through the challenge! If these people are really my friends there is no reason why I can't arrange to see them in places other than bars and pubs. If they are unwilling to make the time then possibly they are not as committed to being friends of mine. If this is the case I can make new friends.'

To dispute Irrational Belief 7: 'How will I ever meet someone to have a relationship with if I can't go to bars? I am lonely and I can't stand it any more. I need a relationship so I must go to the bar in order to find someone to love me!', ask yourself the following questions:

- Is going to the bar really as good a way of finding someone to have a relationship with as I believe? How many hours have I spent standing against a wall drinking in bars and how many women have I actually met? Might it be that bars can be considered a bad place to go looking for someone to have a relationship with because of the nature of the situation?
- Although I am lonely, why can't I stand it any more? Is it possible that I really can stand to be unattached a little longer but that I just do not want to? Am I complaining that I must have what I want right now? Do I believe that I deserve what I want and therefore life must give me someone to love now?
- Rather than complaining and making myself depressed and full of self-pity, how can I solve my problems of finding someone to relate to? Where else besides bars and pubs are good places to go regularly in order to eventually meet someone? What friend or family member might know someone who could be informally introduced to me? Maybe a relationship could develop from there.

- What activities can I engage in to help me cope better with loneliness? If I don't give in and go to the pub, where else can I go to have fun and distract myself from my loneliness and possibly meet someone?
- Do I really need a relationship or just badly want one? What happens when I tell myself I need something that is currently not available to me?
- Will I die if I don't have the relationship that I wrongly think I need?
- How can I stubbornly refuse to make myself miserable about not having a relationship until I find someone to have a relationship with?

Answering these questions will help you to adopt the following rational philosophy: 'I want a romantic relationship, but I do not absolutely need one. I don't need one even if it is true that I am happier when I am involved in a romantic relationship. In order to live, I need oxygen, water and food but I do not absolutely need a romantic relationship. A warm and intimate relationship will make life more enjoyable for me, but it is not an absolute necessity for continuing to live. When I am shopping around to find someone I am compatible with, if I tell myself I absolutely need to find someone, I will make the process that much more difficult. By telling myself I absolutely need someone, I will be quick to conclude that I can't stand the discomfort of living without the pleasure of a relationship. This conclusion will lower my already low discomfort tolerance and increase the chances I will try and soothe myself with alcohol, so I refuse to make it.'

It is far better to tell yourself that you badly want to find someone you can have a warm and loving relationship with so that you can enjoy your life a bit more, but that you don't need such a relationship to be happy. Tell yourself that you really can stand the discomfort of facing life's problems without a relationship and it is good to be able to do this because even if you find someone you have no guarantee you will outlive your lover! Thus, it is good to develop self-reliance so that when

48

you find someone you will not desperately cling to them. People who believe they need their lover rather than want to keep their relationship going because of the pleasure it generates sometimes tend to push away their lover with their emotional dependency. Push yourself not only to give up your dependency on your addiction, but also to learn to be more self-reliant in order to have healthy relationships with friends and lovers. In order to do this, modify the irrational beliefs that make you desperately cling to unhealthy relationships or destroy good relationships with emotional dependency that becomes a burden to your lover.

We hope you can also see that you don't have to go to pubs or bars to find potential lovers and friends. In fact, we believe that there are better places to go to find people to have relationships with. Too often people in bars and pubs do not give you a chance, but rather prematurely judge you on the basis of their immediate reaction to your physical characteristics. For every person you met in a bar or pub you probably had to spend at least 200 hours standing against a wall getting drunk. It seems to us that the only people who profit in this situation are the owner of the bar and the staff who try to make you feel they are your friend so that you buy more drink and tip heavily!

Why not try other strategies to meet people? Each day there are numerous situations where you encounter people, and you can use the method of disputing your irrational beliefs to reduce any anxiety that may make it difficult for you to engage a potential friend or lover in a conversation. Once you have the ability to speak to the potential lover without any addictive substances to reduce your anxiety, you will be able to create opportunities to meet the people you want to meet. Unfortunately, many people falsely believe that they cannot stand the discomfort of breaking the ice and starting a conversation. Some falsely believe that they cannot stand receiving a cold response indicating rejection. However, you can dispute these irrational beliefs and come to see that rejection is unpleasant, but not the end of the world. Getting rejected happens to everyone, and being able to accept yourself unconditionally when a potential lover rejects you is important to being able to live without addiction. Once you unconditionally accept yourself you will feel appropriately sad, disappointed and displeased for not being able to establish the relationship that you want with the person who rejected you. However, with unconditional self-acceptance you will not feel depressed or ashamed for having shown your interest and having been rejected. Unconditional self-acceptance stops you from putting yourself down and rating yourself as not good enough, inadequate, worthless, etc. You can still rate the rejection as bad or undesirable and conclude you are not that person's cup of tea. On the other hand, self-rating leads to self-depreciation which, in turn, leads to self-destruction, because the emotional pain that comes from self-depreciation will enhance your desire for your addiction to escape the pain. But we hope that, as a result of reading this book and pushing yourself to think differently, you will recognize that you can tolerate the discomfort and disappointment of being rejected without having to soothe yourself with drugs, nicotine, pills, food or alcohol! You will see that finding a lover involves learning to try, try and try again to meet people until you find someone who you are compatible with.

In the next chapter, we will address more directly the issue of raising your level of discomfort tolerance.

8

Raise your level of discomfort tolerance

Earlier in this book, we introduced the concept of discomfort tolerance when addressing the importance of persisting at learning how to dispute your self-defeating, irrational beliefs. At this point, we would like to extend discussion of this crucial subject, because if you fail to work on your discomfort tolerance problems it is exceptionally unlikely that you will tolerate life's frequent hassles and obstacles without retreating to the self-destructive comfort of your addiction.

Discomfort tolerance refers to the perceived ability to tolerate discomfort in the many forms that humans experience this unpleasant state. People differ in their ability to tolerate discomfort. A minority of people have general low discomfort tolerance (LDT), while a fortunate few have general high discomfort tolerance (HDT). Most of us, however, have LDT for some events and HDT for others. People with addiction problems tend to have LDT for negative emotions, negative situations, and overcoming their addiction problems. That's the bad news. The good news is that you can raise your level of discomfort tolerance in all of these areas. How can you do this? By following these steps:

Step 1: Recognize the signs of low discomfort tolerance and the consequences of having low discomfort tolerance

Avoidance, lack of persistence for doing what is in your long-term best interest, lack of persistence in thinking through what is better to do, silently or loudly complaining while experiencing feelings like depression, anger, anxiety, self-pity and embarrassment, and, of course, addictive behaviour are all signs that you have problems with low discomfort tolerance. Any decision or action designed to avoid discomfort may

51

suggest the presence of low discomfort tolerance, particularly when it is in your long-term healthy interests to experience and go through discomfort, and when the avoidance of such discomfort is bad for you. A person who decides to leave a slow-moving bank line and use the machine at the bank around the corner is not acting in a way which reflects low discomfort tolerance. This appears to be a rational decision: saving time with no downside is generally good in the long run because you are free then to maximize your satisfaction in life. However, leaving the same bank line because it is slow, knowing full well that if you do not deposit this cheque you will go into the red, is indicative of low discomfort tolerance. It is often the consequences of your actions and decisions that indicate whether you are showing signs of low discomfort tolerance. If your actions are aimed at keeping or making yourself comfortable in the short run but jeopardize your well-being, comfort, safety and satisfaction in the long run, then you are showing signs of having low discomfort tolerance.

Another example of low discomfort tolerance is not making the time or effort to exercise although it will help you stay off addictive substances, help you reduce low back pain and keep your blood pressure, weight and cholesterol within a healthy range. Continuing to smoke cigarettes keeps you comfortable in the here and now but significantly jeopardizes your long-term well-being and is another example of low discomfort tolerance. Failing to do your homework carefully and thus jeopardizing your chances of doing well in a test is still another example of low discomfort tolerance. Not using the principles and practices of Rational Emotive Behaviour Therapy because they are difficult and awkward at first is yet one more example of avoiding doing what is better in the long run and displaying low discomfort tolerance for rational living!

Step 2: Once you have understood how costly your low discomfort tolerance is to your long-term well-being, work diligently at raising your levels of discomfort tolerance so that you can avoid jeopardizing your long-term well-being while maximizing your long-term achievements and satisfaction

In the first chapter of this book, we emphasized the importance of focusing on what you will gain by giving up your addiction, and suggested that you stop focusing on all the present pleasure and comfort you will be missing out on if you do refrain from using your preferred substance. In doing so, we were laying the foundations for the present discussion of discomfort tolerance. The ingredients to human motivation are no mystery. People are motivated in response to their discomfort and comfort. As a human you do have a choice on the comforts you pursue. Rational Emotive Behaviour Therapy is a humanistic therapy because it reminds you that you have free will and the ability to think and reason. By pushing yourself to think about what you are doing by using, say, nicotine, drugs and alcohol you realize that you are creating more discomfort for yourself if you take a careful inventory. Unfortunately, people avoid such objective analysis of their lives and deceive themselves in any number of ways. The well-known support group Narcotics Anonymous has a saying that captures the spirit of our point here. That saying is 'The easiest person to deceive is yourself!' Are you deceiving yourself into wrongly believing that you are not ruining your life every day by continuing with your addiction? Are you deceiving yourself into wrongly believing that the benefits of carrying on the uncomfortable task of learning how to handle both your joys and sorrows without the assistance of your addiction are not worth it? People often don't realize that if they really made a list of all the *costs* their addiction has produced, they could begin to build and sustain motivation for eliminating these harmful habits from their lives. Going over your list on a daily basis, of the *advantages* of giving up will sustain your motivation when you get depressed in response to life. Diligently working on keeping your motivation for the task can be done if you keep your eye on your long-term gains!

Step 3: Search for and record the specific irrational beliefs that you hold and that are responsible for creating your low discomfort tolerance, and all the self-defeating avoidance and substance use that goes along with these irrational beliefs

This is a very important step because you have specific irrational beliefs that we strongly suggest you change if you are going to raise your level of discomfort tolerance. Here are some of the specific irrational beliefs that lead to low discomfort tolerance:

1 People must give me what I want when I want it or else I can't stand it.
2 World conditions must be as I think they absolutely should be or else I can't stand life.
3 I must have certainty in my life. If I don't have certainty I can't stand it.
4 I must have instant success. I can't stand continuing to exert effort to get what I desire if I don't succeed immediately.
5 I must have control over things. I can't stand living with less then perfect control.
6 Life must not have ordinary hassles and I can't stand confronting and coping with the hassles of daily living.
7 Life must not have unusually difficult hassles, tragedies, and obstacles. I wouldn't be able to stand facing any that happen to me.
8 Because life was once easy for me, it absolutely should remain easy and I can't stand this new difficult phase of my life – poor me!
9 It is too hard for me to take responsibility for my self-defeating emotions and behaviours. Thus, I will blame my

parents and the conditions of my life for my self-defeating behaviour.

10 Overcoming my addiction absolutely should be easier and not require so much work, practice and unfamiliar changes in my life. I can't tolerate all this work!

As you identify the specific irrational beliefs and grandiose demands that are at the root of your low discomfort tolerance you prepare yourself for Step 4.

Step 4: Forcefully dispute these specific irrational beliefs, showing yourself that they are illogical, false and self-defeating

Let's look at ways of disputing the above irrational beliefs so that you replace them with more sensible beliefs.

Low Discomfort Tolerance Belief 1: People must give me what I want when I want it or else I can't stand it

Dispute: Why must people give me what I want when I want it?

Answer: They don't have to give me what I want when I want it!

Dispute: Is it really true that I can't stand it when people do not give me what I want when I want it?

Answer: It is not true that I cánnot stand it when people do not give me what I want when I want it. There are plenty of times when I have not received something I really wanted, and if I am honest with myself I realize that all that happened was that I was deprived of the joy, pleasure, comfort or satisfaction of having what I wanted. I am still alive and kicking so I really can stand being deprived, even though of course I do not like to be deprived.

Low Discomfort Tolerance Belief 2: World conditions must be as I think they absolutely should be or else I can't stand life

Dispute: Why must world conditions be as I think they should be?

Answer: World conditions are the way they are. I can insist that things should be better but my insisting does not directly change anything other than making me miserable, depressed, angry, bitter and self-pitying. And, of course, these emotions do not make it easier to cope with difficult world conditions!

Low Discomfort Tolerance Belief 3: I must have certainty in my life. If I don't have certainty I can't stand it

Dispute: Who has certainty in their lives? Where is the evidence that anyone is absolutely certain of the future?

Answer: We all live in a world of probability whether we recognize this fact or not. Perhaps other than the certainty that I will die some day, there is no certainty.

Dispute: Is it true that I can't stand living with uncertainty when in fact I live with uncertainty every day?

Answer: I am wrongly telling myself I can't stand uncertainty when in fact I have stood a great deal of uncertainty each and every day of my life, whether I recognize it or not. So I would tolerate the inherent uncertainty of all aspects of life far better if I recognized that I really can stand uncertainty although I like and prefer certainty!

Low Discomfort Tolerance Belief 4: I must have instant success. I can't stand continuing to exert effort to get what I desire if I don't succeed immediately

Dispute: Obviously I would like instant success, but is it true that I must have it?

Answer: It is not true that I must have instant success just because this is what I want.

Dispute: Is it not closer to the truth that I could choose to stand exerting effort to get what I desire but that I am actually choosing not to exert continued effort towards my goal?

Answer: Yes, this is true. I could stand continuing to exert effort to get what I desire but I am complaining and stopping myself from doing so. This is because I am wrongly demanding that I absolutely should have already achieved my goal given how hard I have worked for it by this point. Unfortunately, regardless of how much effort I believe should be sufficient to achieve my goal, more effort is desired. Tough!

Low Discomfort Tolerance Belief 5: I must have control over things. I can't stand living with less than perfect control

Dispute: Obviously I would like to have control over things but how is it true that I must have control over things?

Answer: I really don't have to have control over things even though I wish I could fully control events. The fact is at best I have some degree of influence over things, people and events. Some people have more influence over certain events, and some people have less influence over certain events, but the fact is no-one has complete control over the things they would like to have control over.

Low Discomfort Tolerance Belief 6: Life must not have ordinary hassles and I can't stand confronting and coping with the hassles of daily living

Dispute: Although it is clear why it would be better if life did not have ordinary hassles, why must life not have such hassles?

Answer: When I think about it there really is no reason why life must not have such ordinary hassles. This is the way life is, a hassle-full experience practically from start to finish. Demanding that life not have such hassles tends to make me emotionally disturbed about such hassles.

Dispute: Although I wish I did not have to be distracted from doing what pleases me, how can it possibly be true that I actually can't stand confronting and coping with the ordinary hassles of life?

Answer: It is not true that I really can't stand coping with hassles, but I wish I did not have to spend my time tending to these things. But if I do, I do.

Low Discomfort Tolerance Belief 7: Life must not have unusually difficult hassles, tragedies and obstacles. I wouldn't be able to stand facing any that happen to me.

Dispute: Why must life not give unusually difficult hassles, tragedies and obstacles?

Answer: Unfortunately, life is not always full of sugar-coated events like a children's story, but rather is sometimes marked by tragedies and very difficult obstacles. I'll be better able to cope with my tragedies if I learn to think rationally about the nature of life!

Low Discomfort Tolerance Belief 8: Because life was once easy for me, it absolutely should remain easy and I can't stand this new difficult phase of my life – poor me!

Dispute: Who says, or where is it written, that because life was once easy it absolutely should remain easy?

Answer: Life is as it is, not how I demand it to be. My grandiose demands for life remaining easy will only make me less able to cope with reality as it is!

Dispute: Why can't I stand this new difficult phase of my life?

Answer: I don't like this difficult phase but I certainly can stand it. If I stop feeling sorry for myself, I will certainly stand this difficult phase of my life far better and can even be somewhat happy despite all the difficulties I face!

Low Discomfort Tolerance Belief 9: It is too hard for me to take responsibility for my self-defeating emotions and behaviours. Thus, I will blame my parents and the conditions of my life for my self-defeating behaviour.

Dispute: Although it is hard to take responsibility for my self-

defeating emotions and behaviours, why must it not
be as difficult as it is?

Answer: Taking responsibility for my own self-defeating
emotions and behaviours is difficult, but if I blame
others for my current predicament it will make it
harder for me to deal with my problem. If I take
responsibility without blaming myself, I will be more
able to help myself.

Low Discomfort Tolerance Belief 10: Overcoming my addiction absolutely should be easier and not require so much work,
practice and unfamiliar changes in my life. I can't tolerate all
this work!

Dispute: Although it would be great if less work and practice
were involved in changing, does it have to be this
way?

Answer: No, overcoming my addiction is difficult and that is
the way it is. If it had to be easier, it would be.

Dispute: I don't want to tolerate all the work and unfamiliar
changes that will be involved in overcoming my
addiction, but does that mean that I can't stand all the
work?

Answer: No. I can stand the hard work and I really won't die
from pushing myself to give up my addiction. On the
other hand, if I don't push myself to stand the hard
work of giving up my addiction then I may very well
die from it!

Step 5: Replace these self-defeating beliefs with new rational beliefs that will lead you to have high discomfort tolerance for uncomfortable and frustrating situations

If you recall, the point of disputing in this area is to create a
new set of high discomfort tolerance beliefs to replace your
low discomfort tolerance beliefs. Here are ten rational beliefs

that you could use to replace the ten low discomfort tolerance beliefs that we have been disputing.

Low Discomfort Tolerance Belief 1: People must give me what I want when I want it or else I can't stand it.

Replacement Belief for High Discomfort Tolerance: I wish people always gave me what I want when I want it but this is generally not the case, and nor does it have to be. I can stand waiting for what I want and I can stand living without getting everything I want.

Low Discomfort Tolerance Belief 2: World conditions must be as I think they absolutely should be or else I can't stand life.

Replacement Belief for High Discomfort Tolerance: I really wish world conditions were as I want them to be. Things would be so much easier and better for everyone. But this is not how reality is, nor unfortunately does it have to be the way I want it to be. I don't like the way life is sometimes, but I really can tolerate it until I die and I will tolerate it better if I see this and choose not to complain about it.

Low Discomfort Tolerance Belief 3: I must have certainty in my life. If I don't have certainty I can't stand it.

Replacement Belief for High Discomfort Tolerance: I would like there to be things in life I can be certain of, but unfortunately we live in a world of probabilities, not certainties. Although I really wish there were more certainty in life, there doesn't have to be and I can tolerate and stand all the uncertainty inherent in life!

Low Discomfort Tolerance Belief 4: I must have instant success. I can't stand continuing to exert effort to get what I desire if I don't succeed immediately.

Replacement Belief for High Discomfort Tolerance: I would much prefer to have instant success in life but it doesn't have to be this way. Very often I will have to work persistently for a long time before I get what I want. I will probably never like this but I can stand continuing to exert effort to get what I desire!

Low Discomfort Tolerance Belief 5: I must have control over things. I can't stand living with less than perfect control.
Replacement Belief for High Discomfort Tolerance: I would really love to have control over things but this is hardly ever possible in life, nor unfortunately does it have to be the way I want it to be. There is so much beyond my direct control in life and I can learn how to stand this fact of reality so that I don't have to numb myself out with drugs, medicines or alcohol. Instead, I will direct my energies to what I can control rather than to what I can't.

Low Discomfort Tolerance Belief 6: Life must not have ordinary hassles, and I can't stand confronting and coping with the hassles of daily living.
Replacement Belief for High Discomfort Tolerance: Life has many ordinary hassles of daily living and there is no law stating that it must be hassle free. Although these hassles may be annoying I really can tolerate confronting them one by one. Life is a series of hassles, obstacles and pleasurable moments, and I will cope with and solve the never-ending parade of challenges of my life if I philosophically accept them and stop my childish complaining!

Low Discomfort Tolerance Belief 7: Life must not have unusually difficult hassles, tragedies and obstacles. I wouldn't be able to stand facing any that happen to me.
Replacement Belief for High Discomfort Tolerance: Life sometimes does have unusually difficult hassles, tragedies and obstacles, and that is tough! I am not immune from these, although I would like to be. I will cope and problem-solve far better if I philosophically accept this and stop moping and start coping!

Low Discomfort Tolerance Belief 8: Because life was once easy for me, it absolutely should remain easy, and I can't stand this new difficult phase of my life – poor me!

Replacement Belief for High Discomfort Tolerance: Because life was once easy for me it doesn't follow that I must be spared difficult phases of life. Unfortunately I have grown accustomed to having things go my way, but I can learn to accustom myself to having it difficult for a while. Telling myself forcefully that I really can stand, tolerate and survive this difficult phase until it ends will help me build my discomfort tolerance in the shortest amount of time.

Low Discomfort Tolerance Belief 9: It is too hard for me to take responsibility for my self-defeating emotions and behaviours. Thus, I will blame my parents and the conditions of my life for my self-defeating behaviour.

Replacement Belief for High Discomfort Tolerance: It is harder in the short term to take responsibility for my self-defeating emotions and behaviours than it is to blame my parents and the conditions of my life for my present problems. However, I would be far better off in the longer term if I did take responsibility for my self-defeating emotions and behaviour. I can stand doing what is more difficult and assume responsibility for my actions. Blaming others for what I do only keeps me addicted!

Low Discomfort Tolerance Belief 10: Overcoming my addiction absolutely should be easier and not require so much work, practice and unfamiliar changes in my life. I can't tolerate all this work!

Replacement Belief for High Discomfort Tolerance: It would be great if overcoming my addiction were easier and did not require so much work, practice and unfamiliar changes in my life, but it does – *tough*! If I stop rebelling against this grim reality and get down to the hard work of getting over my addiction then I will help myself much more than complaining about the hard work and consequently not doing it.

Step 6: Take action and live your life in a away that is consistent with your new high discomfort tolerance beliefs. When you face discomfort, tolerate it rather than run away from it through drug use and you will be living in a way that is consistent with your more rational high discomfort tolerance beliefs

This step is probably the most important step in developing high discomfort tolerance. Rational Emotive Behaviour Therapy is not just an academic exercise in rational thinking. Sometimes people don't make the changes they want to make using REBT because they talk rationally but allow themselves to behave irrationally! As the old expression rightly points out, talk is cheap! The way you behave is the true sign that you are thinking rationally. Someone can say, 'I can stand living without drugs when the going gets rough,' but if most times they face difficulties they find a reason to use their favourite drug one more time, then it is true to say that they have not learned to stand the discomfort of living without drugs. Confront yourself on your tendency to fool and deceive yourself. Do what is uncomfortable and don't settle for rational thinking without constructive action. In common parlance, don't just talk the rational talk, walk the rational walk.

Step 7: Remain vigilant for the human tendency to backslide into low discomfort tolerance. This is an ongoing project to raise your levels of discomfort tolerance so that you remain unaddicted and able to realize your full potential of achievement and satisfaction

This is probably the second most important step if you are going to permanently stay off your addiction and significantly improve your life. Up to this point you probably have had lots of practice at avoiding discomfort by using such things as drugs and alcohol. Since you are so well practised at avoiding discomfort, you will be at risk of backsliding and going back to your addiction. You are human, and you will have a tendency to forget all the pain and trouble it has caused you. Once you have become unaddicted you may take for granted all the progress you have made in stabilizing your life. So, acknowledge that unless you keep on working on maintaining high discomfort tolerance you will easily return to low discomfort tolerance. Just as athletes will get out of shape if they do not continue to train their bodies, you will lose your capacity to tolerate discomfort, thereby setting yourself up to return to the soothing effects of, say, nicotine if you don't do something to keep your discomfort tolerance high. Maintaining high discomfort tolerance is an ongoing process, just as remaining physically fit is an ongoing process. Search for new challenges for your energy. Find and carry out new activities that are uncomfortable but are worth doing in the long run. If you are bored in life, try a new routine. Try a new sport, a new hobby, take a new course or learn a new skill. Realize that your full potential in life goes hand in hand with keeping unaddicted.

In the next chapter, we will consider one particular form of low discomfort tolerance which people who are addicted find especially difficult to tolerate – boredom.

9

Learn to tolerate and deal with boredom

People who report feeling bored often overlook the fact that they get mildly depressed when they are bored. Depression is a very powerful factor that leads to relapse, so it is important that you learn to overcome depression associated with becoming bored. First acknowledge both your boredom and your depression. If you are aware that you are bored and depressed, and you are aware that you are at risk of relapsing, you will be more motivated to take quick action to control your boredom and depression before you turn to drugs and alcohol.

Actively search for any attitudes and beliefs that are leading you to feel depressed about being bored. Here are a few typical self-defeating beliefs.

1 I absolutely should never get bored.
2 Poor me! I need a cigarette (or a drink, or some chocolate) to escape my boredom and if I don't give in to this urge I will get really depressed.
3 Other people don't have my boring life and I must have the good life I see other people enjoying. It's not fair.
4 I have been working so hard to keep off my addiction my efforts absolutely should have paid off in a more rewarding life by now!

We want to emphasize that learning to respond effectively to feelings of boredom and depression is a skill that can be learned. Like all skills it takes practice to acquire. If you have been using addictive substances for years you probably will have to learn these skills, because your answer to boredom has probably been to medicate yourself with your drug or drink of choice. So, accept that it will take some time to learn how to cope with boredom without turning to your addiction but that it can be done. Now let's turn our attention to looking at how to develop the skill of disputing the irrational beliefs that we have just listed.

Irrational Belief 1: I absolutely should never get bored

Dispute: Where is it written that I absolutely should never get bored?

Answer: Nowhere other than my head! I wish I never became bored, but I am not exempt from boredom. This sometimes will occur. Too bad! I will accept that boredom occasionally occurs and will go and experiment with ways to alleviate or tolerate it.

Irrational Belief 2: Poor me! I need a cigarette (or a drink, or some chocolate) to escape my boredom and if I don't give in to this urge I will get really depressed.

Dispute: Yes, I do want these things to escape my boredom, but do I need them?

Answer: No, I really just want them but don't absolutely need them.

Additional Dispute: If I don't escape the boredom by turning to my addiction, must I get really depressed?

Answer: No. I can choose to be bored, and accept I am bored and not make myself depressed over being bored. This takes work but it is possible. Now, how can I push myself to stop getting depressed and what can I do to alleviate my boredom?

Irrational Belief 3: Other people don't have my boring life, and I must have the good life I see other people enjoying. It's not fair.

Dispute: Where is the evidence that I must have the good life I see other people enjoying? Where is it written that life is supposed to be fair?

Answer: There is no strong, objective evidence to conclude that I must have the good life I see other people enjoying. In fact, quite the contrary. Life is unfair:

some people are given good things, some people work for them, and some people never get good things because they don't take action, are not talented or are unlucky. I can complain about this unfairness until the cows come home or I can accept what I can't change and try my best to change what I can!

Irrational Belief 4: I have been working so hard to stay clean and sober my efforts absolutely should have paid off in a more rewarding life by now!

Dispute: Things could be this way but do they have to turn out as they 'ideally should'?

Answer: No, they don't. Unfortunately, life can be very unfair and difficult! Too bad. Now, if I keep working at staying clean and sober sooner or later things will get better. Sooner or later my efforts will pay off. Sooner or later I will have a more rewarding life. Complaining won't make it happen any sooner and will put me back to my addiction. So I will hang in there and keep working and tolerating the discomfort!

We suggest you spend a good deal of time preparing for boredom by making a list of activities you can do when you begin to get bored. When bored, the urge to return to your addiction may be so strong you won't be able to think of much else other than the predictable comfort of intoxication. So make that list and have it handy for when the urge strikes. Here is a sample list.

Activities to counter boredom

1 Rent a video (drama, inspirational or humorous).
2 Take exercise – walk, run, row, lift, cycle, swim.
3 Sing.
4 Learn to sing.
5 Learn to do anything you don't already know how to do and want to do.

6 Practise any skill you are mediocre at so you become an expert.
7 Play music or make music.
8 Go to a museum or a zoo.
9 Cook a special meal.
10 Plan a trip.
11 Read a book.
12 Visit a bookshop.
13 Go to a coffee bar.
14 Call a friend.
15 Read the newspaper.
16 Write a letter to a friend.
17 Write in your diary or journal.
18 Clean your house.
19 Take a leisurely walk.
20 Go window-shopping.
21 Re-read this fine book!
22 Write the authors of this book a letter outlining your experiences in using our principles.
23 Garden, learn to garden, visit a garden.
24 Start any non-destructive activity and stick with it until the boredom goes away.
25 Write your own book.
26 Water your plants.
27 Mow your lawn.
28 Offer to mow your neighbour's lawn.
29 Learn how to write.
30 Attend to your finances.
31 Put all your photos in photo albums.
32 Throw out all the junk you have in your house and organize your space.

Of all the items in the above list, perhaps the most important recommendation is 24, which is to start any non-destructive activity and stick with it until the boredom goes away. Experiment with this piece of advice and see for yourself how effective it is!

In addition to disputing your irrational beliefs that make you depressed and having handy a list of activities you can do when bored, simultaneously dispute the irrational beliefs that will stop you doing something healthy to alleviate your boredom. Here are two important beliefs that will keep you wallowing in your boredom:

1 It is too hard to get my list of activities to alleviate my boredom and start doing one of them.
2 I can't stand getting up and starting any non-destructive activity and sticking with it until the boredom goes away!

Let's look at how you could attempt to dispute these two irrational beliefs that will keep you stuck in your inactivity and boredom:

Irrational Belief 1: It is too hard to get my list of activities to alleviate my boredom and start doing one of them

Dispute: Is it really too hard or am I just telling myself that? If someone offered to give me £500 to go and find my list, would it still be beyond me and too hard?

Answer: *No*! I am just telling myself it is too hard to go and get that list. Let me push myself and start to get that list now! I can do it!

Irrational Belief 2: I can't stand getting up and starting any non-destructive activity and sticking with it until the boredom goes away!

Dispute: Is it that I can't stand or just don't feel inclined to start any non-destructive activity and stick with it until the boredom goes away?

Answer: I don't feel inclined to start any non-destructive activity, but I really could stand the discomfort of doing so if I chose to.

In addition to challenging the irrational beliefs that block you from trying to do some healthy activity to alleviate your

69

boredom, also attack those self-defeating thoughts and beliefs tempting you to pursue the high of your addictive activity. Here are two such examples:

Irrational Belief 3: I am bored and I need my addiction and I must give in to this urge

Dispute: Will I die if I refuse to give in to this urge? Do I need, say, drugs and alcohol or do I want the temporary feeling they will give me?

Answer: I will not die if I refuse to take drugs and alcohol, but I may very well go back to being addicted if I relapse! I certainly want the relief that drugs and alcohol will yield, but I won't perish from boredom. I want immediate relief but I don't absolutely need it. I can tolerate this boredom and then deal with it without using drugs or drink.

Irrational Belief 4: I can't stand this internal fight against my addiction any longer!

Dispute: Is it true that I can't stand fighting my urges?

Answer: Certainly not. Indeed, I will gain a great deal the longer I fight. If I am honest with myself I know that my addiction keeps me back in life in so many ways. Addiction is a bottomless pit and a dead-end alley. The internal fight is a struggle, but if I take it minute by minute and hang in their the beast of addiction may go back to sleep and leave me alone. I can stand the discomfort. I will take control of the beast of addiction, and now let me go and distract myself in some healthy way, like exercising!

So, as you can see, we recommend that you learn to both tolerate and deal with boredom. Boredom is a threat to progress, and learning skills to structure your free time so that you don't get the chance to think about doing drugs, smoking or using alcohol is important. Practise thinking ahead and plan activities to do on your own and with non-drug-abusing friends for your free time after work and on the weekends. Learn to think ahead and plan how you will spend each hour on the weekends and evenings. This will take some effort but the more you practise making plans and structuring your free time the better chance you will have of avoiding boredom. And when boredom sneaks in, despite your greatest efforts and best-laid plans, use your ability to think rationally to gracefully tolerate your bored moments. Relapse often happens during periods of boredom. So plan ahead to prevent boredom, and fight the good fight if it takes you by surprise. You really can stand the discomfort of boredom!

10

Develop unconditional self-acceptance

Virtually all humans have a self-defeating habit of rating themselves, their essences or their personal worth. From the day you are born, you tend to be given a global rating. As you grow up you learn to make similar ratings of yourself, and the emotional consequences of this habit can be disastrous.

It is so common to hear a parent or a teacher say, 'Johnny, you are such a good boy,' just after the child does something good. The child's action is good, and the parent or teacher in this case decides to rate Johnny as a good boy on the basis of his action. Of course, Johnny does not dislike this rating of his boyhood or personhood because he has received a positive rating and feels good about himself.

Because Johnny is a fallible human it is inevitable that he will use poor judgement and do something bad. It is equally common in this situation to hear an adult say, 'Johnny, you are a bad boy,' just after he has violated some cultural or social rule. The child's action is bad and the adult decides to rate Johnny as a bad boy on the basis of his action. Johnny, in all probability, is troubled by this negative rating of his personhood. He probably will feel either guilty, ashamed or depressed, or some combination of all these feelings.

In tone and manner, directly and indirectly, children are taught to rate their worth on the basis of their actions, achievements, judgements and abilities, as well as their physical characteristics. Adults teach children to do this because, in all probability, these adults are predisposed to sloppy reasoning and from their point of view this approach to reprimanding a child makes perfect sense. This type of rating happens many, many times and becomes automatic to children and adults. Without too much effort you have learned to feel good about yourself when you do well and bad about yourself when you do poorly.

This tendency to rate yourself on the basis of your actions

and decisions is what we in Rational Emotive Behaviour Therapy call making global self-ratings. Because you are probably so well practised at giving yourself a global self-rating it may be difficult for you to stop this emotionally harmful practice. However, it will greatly help you to overcome your addiction if you learn to put into practice the principles of self-acceptance outlined in this chapter and minimize your tendency to globally rate your essence or personhood on the basis of how well you act or your progress towards reaching your goals.

The main reason global self-ratings are a problem is because they create strong feelings of shame, guilt and depression which greatly interfere with you making psychological and behavioural changes. Such changes take a good deal of work and practice to achieve because to some extent human nature resists change even for the better. When you fail at quickly making the psychological and behavioural changes you hope to make, the global self-ratings you assign to your essence will significantly interfere with you working to overcome your addiction. Look at the following five beliefs and consider whether you have ever thought about yourself in such terms:

1 I am useless because I have failed so many times to kick my addiction.
2 I am worthless because I have this problem with addiction.
3 I am an addict and that makes me a failure compared to my high-achieving brother.
4 I am not as good as all the other recovering addicts because I am weak and I often relapse.
5 I am a fool for allowing drugs (or alcohol, or nicotine, or tranquillizers, or bingeing) to ruin my life.

Although some of you may quickly acknowledge that globally rating your essence or self leads to harmful and painful emotions, others may resist acknowledging that this way of thinking is counterproductive. Often, we find people have difficulty with these concepts because they think that if they stop their global self-ratings they will somehow be condoning drug use or other kinds of harmful or wrong behaviour. The truth is that you can hold yourself responsible for your negative behaviours without globally rating your self or essence.

You are responsible for your actions and decisions. Because you are responsible for what you do when you are high or intoxicated, you and only you will face the consequences of your actions. But it is important for you to face the consequences of your irresponsible drug, nicotine or alcohol use *without* shame, guilt or depression. These emotions make it harder for you to acknowledge that you have a problem. The denial that is so common in those who abuse various substances comes from the shame, guilt, fear and depression that people with addictions would consciously feel if they acknowledged their addiction problem. Denying your problem only allows it to get worse, and the more well practised you are at escaping your emotions with addiction the harder it will be to change your coping skills. Learning to accept yourself as a fallible, unrateable human being with a problem of addiction will help you to drop your denial and to own up to your problem.

The alternative to giving yourself a global self-rating is to rate only your actions, decisions and other dimensions of your personality while unconditionally accepting yourself as a whole. This means that you rate something you do as good or bad in the context of your goals, while not rating yourself as a person as being good or bad. People find this very hard to do. However, if you teach yourself to do this you will not experience the strong negative feelings about yourself that rob you of the motivation for continuing to learn how to eliminate your addiction. With unconditional self-acceptance you can responsibly look at the things you did to set yourself up to use your chosen substance without the shame and guilt that makes you want to give up trying to overcome your problem.

People often find it easier to accept themselves conditionally. In fact, all of the five statements listed above are the kinds of things people think to themselves when they have conditional self-acceptance and violate the conditions under which they will accept themselves. These five statements are examples of the self-depreciation that people do when they violate the conditions under which they will accept themselves. Let's examine each of the five examples for the conditions that have been violated.

In *Example 1*: 'I am useless because I have failed so many times to kick my addiction,' the condition for worth is kicking addiction. This person will think well of herself (in this case) if she is not using but puts herself down as being 'useless' because she has failed to kick her habit. If she were to develop unconditional self-acceptance she could think, 'It is bad to relapse for many different reasons and I will set myself up for certain negative consequences for having relapsed. Nevertheless, relapsing doesn't make me less of a person. Regardless of whether I succeed or fail I am never useless. I am a fallible human being who either does well or poorly and frequently a mixture of the two.'

In *Example 2*: 'I am worthless because I have this problem with addiction,' the condition for worth is not having a problem with addiction. This person will feel worthwhile if and only if he (in this case) eliminates his problem with addiction. Of course, since he is struggling to learn the necessary skills to get over his problem he is feeling worthless, because he doesn't see how to think about himself otherwise. He also may not see how his worthless feelings actually interfere with him accomplishing his primary goal of learning how to overcome his addiction. If this person were to minimize his bad habit of globally rating himself, he could think, 'Having this problem with addiction is bad because it interferes with the quality of my life but I am neither bad nor worthless as a person because I have this problem. How can I learn what it takes to now get over the problem?' Thinking this way reflects unconditional self-acceptance: the person would feel concerned and frustrated about his addiction, but not worthless about himself as a person.

In *Example 3*: 'I am an addict and that makes me a failure compared to my high-achieving brother', the condition for self-esteem is acting more like the person's high-achieving brother. This person globally rates herself (in this case) both as an addict and as a failure when comparing her behaviour to the behaviour exhibited by her high-achieving brother. Comparing your behaviour with another person's behaviour is fine. Making this comparison helps you to learn how your behaviour is similar or different, better or worse, compared to another person's behaviour. Comparing your behaviour to that of another person helps you learn how to improve your behaviour. However, going beyond comparing behaviour and rating your essence and the essence or personhood of your brother as a result of this behavioural comparison leads to emotional problems. Concluding that you are a failure because your behaviour is inferior to that of your brother will make you feel so bad that you won't work to improve your behaviour. Rather, you may well go back to your addiction to soothe your feelings of inferiority.

Instead, it is recommended that you say to yourself, 'I have an addiction and because of it I sometimes fail at achieving my goals. My brother tends to achieve many of his goals and that is good for him. If I really want to achieve some of my goals like my brother I would do better to unconditionally accept myself while objectively rating addictive behaviour as counter-productive to my goals.'

In *Example 4*: 'I am not as good as all the other recovering addicts because I am weak and I often relapse', this person is using a record of abstinence as the condition for her (in this case) self-esteem. She will feel good if she behaves strongly and resists the urge to relapse. Unfortunately, even the most hard-working individuals sometimes relapse, because over-coming an addiction is difficult and complex. Relapse can be rationally viewed as a way of learning how to get sober or clean. If you rate the relapse as not good but helpful for learning, and you continue to accept yourself unconditionally even after having a relapse, you will not get so hopeless and down on yourself and you will work to understand what you could have done to prevent the relapse. So instead of thinking that you are not as good as the other recovering addicts because you have relapsed, draw a distinction between your skills at abstinence and your self-worth. Try saying to yourself, 'I am acceptable as a person even though I have relapsed. My relapse is not good and it suggests my skills are not sufficient for remaining free. Now, how can I learn new skills so I won't relapse next time under similar conditions?' This self-accepting belief will help you to continue to search for the understanding that will take you to a life without addiction.

In *Example 5*: 'I am a fool for allowing drugs (or alcohol, or nicotine, or tranquillizers, or bingeing) to ruin my life', the person is rating himself (in this case) as a fool because he has violated his condition of self-esteem. The implicit condition of self-esteem is to not ruin your life. This philosophy is that 'I am OK if I don't ruin my life and I am not OK if I ruin my life.' Unfortunately, this attitude will make you feel so bad about the past that you won't be emotionally prepared to salvage the future. Why not try unconditional self-acceptance and acknowledge that it was a foolish thing to do to let, say, alcohol use have such a negative impact on your life? Unfortunately, fallible humans do some very foolish things like this! Calling yourself a fool won't help you to stop your foolish ways! Acknowledge your unwise decisions and behaviours. Work on changing your ways, but avoid labelling yourself as a fool. Instead, accept yourself as a fallible, unrateable, complex human being who can act foolishly and non-foolishly.

If you recognize that you have a definite problem with self-acceptance, we suggest that you read *How to Accept Yourself* by Dr Windy Dryden (Sheldon Press, 1999).

Self-acceptance is an important cornerstone of mental health. There are others, and these are discussed in the next chapter.

11

Develop a mentally healthy approach to life

Overcoming your addiction problems can be quite a confusing challenge. There are many skills you will have to develop to successfully handle all the stress and temptation you encounter in today's complex world. Your efforts to overcome your addiction and lead a happier life require a blueprint. In this chapter, we offer you fifteen recommendations that could be viewed as a healthy approach to life. Let's look at each of the fifteen recommendations and see how you would implement them into your systematic efforts to overcome your addictions and improve the quality of your life.

Develop healthy self-interest

In order to successfully overcome your addiction you will have to develop a good deal of healthy self-interest. It is recommended that you put yourself first and everyone else a close second. One problem some individuals with addictions have is that they are people-pleasers who don't put themselves first but instead put others first. Their drug and alcohol use may help them over-extend themselves so that they can keep other people happy and comfortable. Sacrificing yourself occasionally for those for whom you care is fine, but it is best not to overdo your sacrifice for other people. If you are going to beat your addiction you are going to have to lead your life differently. Perhaps you will have to make more time for yourself in order to reduce stress and regain the vitality you desire naturally without having to turn to your addiction. Maybe you will have to move closer to your job because you have been commuting long hours and miles to work each day and you are finally realizing that you are not Superman and need time to jog, rest or be with your family instead of only working, commuting and sleeping. Such a change might mean that others in your family might be a little uncomfortable as you either take a job closer to home for less money or move closer to your job and give up the serenity and space of the suburbs. Of course, this would not be an easy thing to do, but very often substance-abusing individuals are unrealistic with respect to how to pace their lives. And the substances allow them to put up with an unrealistic schedule or commute each day at the expense of their long-term health and happiness.

People will sometimes reject this recommendation out of guilt. The irrational belief they hold leading to this self-defeating guilt is 'I must put others first and myself second – so says my culture, my parents, etc.' You can challenge this belief and see that there is nothing wrong with putting yourself first and others a close second. In fact, if you put yourself first and get over your addiction, you probably will function far better in your role as a parent, spouse, son or daughter than you do when you have an active addiction. Indeed, when you have an addiction, the addiction is what is in control of your life. Feeding your addiction is what comes first, and all else second.

How do you go about learning to put yourself first and others a close second? You use your best judgement and give up your demands for perfection. You work at unconditionally accepting yourself even if others criticize you for putting yourself first and everyone else a close second. You dispute your irrational belief about gaining approval from significant others and you work at approving your own efforts to judge what is best to do to overcome your addiction. And realize that there are paradoxes in life. Some of the time you may put others first. For example, if you are fair with your spouse and sometimes compromise and put her (in this case) first she will in all probability be more likely to put you first sometimes, and you will be setting the stage for a good relationship. Putting yourself first sometimes means doing nice things for others, who will then be more inclined in the future to do nice things for you. So avoid being dogmatic about putting yourself first and others a close second. This is a guideline that you can strive to implement in your life over the long run.

Last, as you work on giving up your addiction, some of the people who profited from your addiction may try to convince you to give up on your quest for sobriety. For example, your drinking 'friends' will try to convince you to join them, or your so-called 'friend' the drug-dealer will try to tempt you to come by and visit because he has not seen you for a long time. Don't back off from your commitment to put yourself first and others a close second. Confidently tell them that you are firm in your resolve to learn to live life without drugs or alcohol, or whatever your chosen substance may be, because you have reached the decision that at least for you these substances create more problems than the pleasure they bring!

Develop social interest

Because we live in a social world it is adaptive to respect other people's rights and to assist them when possible. If you have little or no regard for those with whom you live it is likely that they will have little or no interest in respecting your right to live well and happily. Therefore, social interest is a form of healthy self-interest. Understand that just because you have decided to overcome your addiction everyone else in your social world still has their own goals, problems and desires that they too are striving to face. It is not uncommon for people who are working to give up their addiction to demand that their family support them fully in the way that the individual defines. Sometimes this broad definition of support includes expecting family members not to hold them responsible for carrying out basic chores around the house. Remember that just because you have decided to overcome your addiction the world doesn't stop. Be reasonable with the people you live and work with and be interested in their well-being as you are striving to overcome your problems. If you fail to have social interest as you pursue your own interests you will have interpersonal conflicts that will sooner or later add to the stresses and tension in your life. Interpersonal stress and strife will put you at risk of relapse, so you will have to improve your skills at learning to balance your self-interest with the interests of the people you live and work with. This is what is meant by healthy social interest.

It is also recommended that you recognize that there is only so much you can do for other people, and it is sometimes wise to allow others to make mistakes and face the consequences of their misjudgements. So let us caution you against becoming zealously socially interested. Too much of a good thing is no good. If you try and save other people from the consequences of their indulgence you are enabling them to avoid life's consequences. The consequences of life help us to learn what is good to do and what is best avoided. So watch overdoing social interest. Help people and be interested, but don't cross the fine line between healthy social interest and neurotic over-involvement.

Learn self-direction

Well-adjusted people accept responsibility for their own lives. They identify what brings them pleasure and meaning and pursue it by primarily, but not exclusively, relying on their own efforts, judgements and resources. If you are going to overcome your problems with addiction you will have to learn how to be self-directed. It is important that you realize that, as a person who was addicted, you were directed by your drug or drink of choice. Overcoming your addiction requires that you discover and experiment with becoming independent and self-directed. Rather than blame external factors or circumstances for your addiction, accept full responsibility for choosing to use drugs, nicotine, booze or whatever it may be. It is true that some people may have tempted you or encouraged you to continue with your addiction. But you will not overcome it and reap all the benefits that go with doing so if you place too much emphasis on other people or external conditions. Identify your own coping strategies for avoiding people, places and things which tempt you to continue. You and only you have the greatest to gain by staying sober or clean and the most to lose by being addicted, because this is your life. Accept that you will have to direct yourself and experiment with new ways of finding pleasure and meaning instead of relying on your old friend – intoxication. It will be difficult at first to learn to be self-directed. You may not even want to admit that you lack self-direction and need help in this area of your life. However, drop your defensiveness and really examine in what ways you are following others and not being self-directed.

Don't expect to learn how to be self-directed overnight, nor expect to discover all the skills to cope with stress and temptation in a few months. Accept that learning to avoid your addictive substance will take a long time, but through it all you will be in the driver's seat of your life. Experiment with self-direction and there is a good chance that you will lead yourself to sobriety and all the benefits it will eventually bring.

Develop high discomfort tolerance (HDT)

As we showed you in Chapter 8, having high discomfort tolerance will help you to act in your long-term interests even when it is uncomfortable to do so. You will also need HDT to get over your addiction. Push yourself to work on raising your level of discomfort tolerance. Avoid copping out and saying to yourself that change is too difficult. Raising your level of discomfort tolerance is difficult, but not *too* difficult. The benefits of slowly but surely working on your discomfort tolerance problems will be great. With a high discomfort tolerance you will be able to accomplish other goals besides overcoming your addiction. Achievement requires high discomfort tolerance. Accept this and you will be well on your way to achieving your most cherished goals!

Be flexible

People who adapt well to this world show flexibility and the ability to survive and cope with changing circumstances. They avoid complaining about the changing circumstances of life.

As a person addicted to, say, cigarettes or drink, you show how inflexible you are every time you turn to these substances to cope with your frustrations. Your method of coping is limited to one response – get intoxicated and escape. Overcoming your addiction will involve learning how to solve your problems in a flexible manner. This skill will require some practice, and you won't learn to be flexible overnight. Dispute your irrational beliefs that keep you from becoming more flexible in your response to life's ups and downs. Push yourself to grow. You will find that becoming flexible is uncomfortable, but the more you push yourself to tolerate the discomfort of being flexible the more you will develop this coping skill.

Try being flexible when it comes to using your free time. Instead of just doing nothing, experiment with new activities that you can afford. Don't use lack of money or your age as an excuse for remaining inflexible. Find new ways to have fun instead of relaxing with your joint or junk food. The more flexible you become, the greater your chances of overcoming your addiction and enjoying life despite its difficult hassles.

Learn to accept uncertainty

Individuals who cope well accept that we live in a probabilistic world where absolute certainty does not exist. Therefore, they accept that judgements and decisions can be made with no guarantee that things will work as planned. Mature, effective people make their decisions based on incomplete knowledge, and responsibly cope with the outcomes of their decisions and learn from each one so as to increase their knowledge for future decisions.

In order to successfully overcome your addiction it is very important that you improve your skills for tolerating uncertainty. Addictive substances provide a safe haven from your worries and fears, albeit a very temporary one. If you are going to get more skilled at dealing with these worries and fears, you will have to get comfortable with the uncertainties of life.

Keep your rational preference for knowing that you will be safe and that things will go your way, but give up those anxiety-creating demands for certainty. Also, give up those demands for guarantees, because there are (almost certainly) no guarantees in life! We really wish there were, but about the only one we can think of is that we are all going to die – and even this might change in the future! So since we have no choice but to live in a world of probabilities, why not learn to accept uncertainty? Gain comfort from probabilities (e.g. working hard greatly increases the probability of succeeding at any chosen endeavour, so work hard if you really, really, really want something).

Commit yourself to creative pursuits

People tend to be healthier and happiest when they have vitally absorbing interests. Such interests give life meaning and lead people to structure their time to achieve their long-term goal. Examples of such vitally absorbing interests include raising children, writing books, political activism, discovery of new knowledge, social service, gardening, creating art, research and development, investing, etc.

We can't emphasize enough how important it is to find creative pursuits when you are looking to overcome your addiction. When you decide to seriously work on giving up, you are essentially deciding to restructure a very large part of your life. In order to do this you had better find something to do with your time, energy and money. If you are going to revamp your life in this way you are going to have to find meaning in life without your addiction. Getting high, smoking or eating was a time-consuming endeavour. It helped you meet people, gave you something to look forward to, and helped you escape from the boredom of everyday living. Part of overcoming your addiction had better include other creative pursuits that will also help you meet people, give you something to look forward to, and help you escape from the boredom of everyday living. The key to finding creative pursuits is to experiment with new activities! Don't cop out and believe you are too in debt to try new things. If an activity that costs you a little money helps you overcome your addiction, it will be more than cost-effective in the long run. And don't let your shame or fear block you from experimenting with new activities. We all start out as beginners when we begin something new! So accept that at first you will fumble a little with the new activity until it becomes reinforcing and fun. Don't demand instant gratification to stop you from trying new things. You may have to give certain activities a chance before they grab you the way that your addiction did. Push yourself to find those new activities and to keep on finding new creative pursuits. What grabs you during the first six months of your plan to overcome your addiction won't necessarily be as fulfilling after you are six years into your abstinence. People very often react well to new endeavours. So keep on trying new sports, writing new articles and books, developing new skills, or taking up new causes! Pursue meaning in life rather than sitting on your heels and waiting for meaning and fulfilment to come your way.

Think scientifically

Individuals with minimal emotional disturbance achieve this through the use of logic and scientific thinking. Employing scientific thinking, these people tend to adapt to life through regulating their emotions and actions by reflecting on them and evaluating their consequences in terms of the extent to which they lead to short-term and long-term goals. Individuals who are well adjusted tend to avoid overgeneralizing about other people and life in general. They tend to avoid black-and-white categorical thinking and view things along a spectrum. Finally, they tend to have an experimental approach to life and create hypotheses and carefully look for evidence that disproves their hypothetical beliefs.

This entire book is an effort to teach you how to think scientifically and use the methods of science and logic to help you overcome your addictions. Instead of believing that it is too hard to learn to think differently, focus your efforts on trying to implement these methods in whatever way you can. The more you practise thinking scientifically the better you will get at it. Avoid labelling yourself a 'stupid drug addict' or a 'hopeless drunk', a 'helpless pill-popper' or a 'pathetic smoker', because that is an example of black-and-white thinking that will block you from feeling motivated to develop the skills for overcoming your addiction. Don't make what is called the 'Fortune Teller Error' and predict that you can't change because you have failed in the past. Just because you have failed simply means you failed in the past. You could very well succeed in the future because you are trying again with the knowledge of what went wrong last time you failed at giving up. Like a scientist, make a hypothesis that it is possible that with sufficient work and practice you can overcome your addiction. And, like a good scientist, put this hypothesis to the test many, many times!

Accept yourself unconditionally

People who are well adjusted tend to accept themselves unconditionally and avoid rating their essence, personal worth or self. They rate their actions in reference to their goals. They rate aspects of themselves like their traits, qualities, skills, talents, etc., but avoid coming up with a total score or label which rates their totality. Well-adjusted people acknowledge that they are complex and ever-changing beings who cannot be objectively rated in totality. With this philosophy these well-adjusted people live life to enjoy themselves rather than to prove themselves.

We previously devoted an entire chapter to this incredibly important concept. What bears repeating here is that although it is very unfamiliar and difficult to give up the bad habit of rating your essence and having conditional self-acceptance, the benefits of developing unconditional self-acceptance are very significant! Responsibly acknowledge your poor judgements and negative deeds, but push yourself to accept yourself unconditionally with no ifs, ands or buts! This will aid you in your future attempts to correct your poor judgements and bad behaviour.

Take calculated risks

Humans who are well adjusted take calculated risks to increase their chances of attaining their goals. They avoid impulsive or poorly evaluated risks and tend to prefer considering the long- and short-term advantages to any course of action. Such individuals tend to be adventurous without being foolhardy.

If you are going to overcome your self-defeating addiction problems you will have to learn to take calculated risks. Even your efforts to overcome your addictions are a calculated risk. To succeed at this change you will have to risk much effort, time and energy and you have no certainty of your eventual success. However, if you remain addicted the probability is very high that the problems will continue to mount. You are very likely to end up totally destroying your family, your job prospects and your health. When you evaluate all that is on the line, doing all the hard work involved in giving up an addiction seems like a very good calculated risk to take.

As an individual who abuses an addictive substance you probably are quite impulsive. The low discomfort tolerance that contributed to your addiction was also probably responsible for poorly thought-out decisions and actions. If you are going to succeed in overcoming your addiction and significantly improve the quality of your life, it is important that you work on learning to give up impulsiveness and only take calculated risks. Tolerate the discomfort of waiting and thinking about what you at first feel like doing. Carry out homework assignments to practise waiting and evaluating whether a given course of action is a good risk. For example, I (Walter Matweychuk) will often wish to buy a book when I am browsing in a bookshop. But I have learned to stand the discomfort of not immediately buying it and first reviewing the table of contents. Then I leave the shop and think about buying it over the next couple of days or weeks. If, after a few days, I come to see that I really want the book and it would be a good investment to have, I go back to the bookshop and buy the book. This way I have given myself time to calculate whether I am really likely to read this new book. You too could stand the discomfort of doing a similar type of exercise. When you want to buy a dress, a new suit or anything else you like, think through your decision and sleep on it. You will be building your discomfort tolerance for waiting to act and deciding if purchasing the item is a good calculated risk to take.

Other calculated risks you may want to consider taking involve investing in education, finding a Rational Emotive Behaviour Therapist and sincerely working on overcoming your addiction, or saving your money, seeking the advice of a financial planner and investing it to improve your long-term financial security. You may want to experiment with new ways of enjoying yourself, new sports and hobbies, even if they involve spending some money. The risk-taking involves the fact that you may never use the equipment you buy, but on the other hand sports and other hobbies are better ways of spending your free time than on your addiction.

Last, you may want to consider calculated risks in the areas of work and love. Are you satisfied with your job and career? Would it be a good long-term decision to move in a different direction with your career? It may be that you will have to go back to school, and that is expensive, but the risk may be worth it. And with your relationship: is it time to either improve your love relationship or end it and move on? It is risky when you change what is familiar, but would it be a good risk, all things considered? Think carefully about such changes before you act. You can stand the discomfort in order to carefully calculate what is a good risk to take and a bad risk to avoid. As with nearly all other skills, the more you try to evaluate risk and take only good calculated risks, the better you will become at it. And if you later learn your evaluation was faulty and you took a bad risk, work hard to accept yourself unconditionally with your poor decision and learn from it. Mistakes are opportunities to learn and identify in what ways you overlooked things that could have led to a far better decision, so next time you will be better prepared.

Adopt the philosophy of long-range hedonism

Hedonism is the philosophy of pleasure-seeking, and the hedonist is one who devotes their life to the pursuit of pleasure. There are two kinds of hedonism – long-term hedonism and short-term hedonism. As a person who is misusing and is addicted to, say, drugs and alcohol, you are practising the self-defeating philosophy of short-term hedonism. Your substance use makes you feel comfortable for the moment at the expense of your long-term well-being.

As part of your effort to overcome your addiction, acknowledge how self-defeating short-term hedonism really is. Be balanced and learn to seek both short-term pleasures and long-term achievements. Live for both today and tomorrow, without jeopardizing tomorrow for the comforts and pleasures of today. Of course, this means giving up such things as alcohol or bingeing because you realise how detrimental they are to so many different aspects of your long-term well-being. Again, your family, career, financial security and health are all at risk in the long run as you continue with your addiction. Maximize your happiness with an appreciation of the future consequences of today's actions. You will have some discomfort in the short run if you push yourself to give up. However, ever so slowly but steadily the balance will shift, and the short-term discomfort will be reduced and the long-term gains will begin to occur. Slowly, your head will clear and you will think more clearly. Slowly, your relationships will become less problematic and you will learn to handle people and your problems with them in a more effective way. Slowly, you will feel more confident that it surely is worth your effort to stick with the process of living and enjoying life without addiction. You will realize that your happiness is greater as you liberate yourself from the slavery of being an addict!

Develop an outlook of non-Utopianism

Individuals who are well adjusted realize that Utopias are not likely to exist. They have ideals in mind that they use as goals and guides to work towards. However, they also choose to avoid upsetting themselves by being realistic and accepting that it is unlikely that a state of perfect achievement, health, comfort, etc., can ever be achieved.

Giving up your addiction will also involve becoming more realistic about life. You will have to work on the rigid idealism, perfectionism and other inflexible, but romantic, ways of looking at life that can contribute to you becoming depressed, hopeless, bitter, angry and despairing when life is not ideal as you think it absolutely should be. As you get more realistic about what being addicted has done to you, your health and your family life, you will be motivated to stay unaddicted.

Push yourself to be and to stay realistic. The denial that is so common to drug use is maintained by avoiding realistic thinking. Convince yourself that it is not too uncomfortable to be realistic. Accept life as it is rather than demanding that it must be one endless party with all pleasure and no work! There is no evidence that realism will hurt you. Being realistic helps you to plan for your future and to protect yourself. Certainly this does not mean not having personal aspirations. Keep your preferences and strive to achieve them. But accept in a realistic way that you will have to work hard to get things that you really want. Don't think that changing must be easy and perfectly achieved. Use the methods imperfectly that we have outlined in this book as a way of learning how to get better and better at using them. Push yourself to go without drugs, alcohol, pills, cigarettes and comfort eating. If you slip after a period of abstinence don't give up and demand that you be perfect. Just analyse how you could have done things differently in order to maintain your freedom. Analyse what you have to do in order to start another period of abstinence, and then get going. Remember, you are a fallible person, and if at first you don't succeed try, try, try again until you achieve your goal!

Take responsibility for your own emotional disturbance

Individuals who are well adjusted tend to accept responsibility for their own emotional disturbance rather than defensively blaming others or social conditions for their self-defeating thoughts, feelings and behaviour. If you are going to overcome your addiction you are going to have to stop blaming any external source for it, and acknowledge that you choose to get upset and then cop out and take drugs, smoke or drink to feel better.

Adopt a healthy lifestyle

Individuals who are well adjusted creatively attempt to find the proper balance between work, play, rest, exercise and leisure activities to produce optimal physical and psychological functioning. They are concerned about maintaining their vitality and monitor their eating patterns, as well as their exercise status and typical resting rituals. Such individuals take time to maintain their body rather than living for the comforts of the moment and risking disease and poor quality of life in the future.

If you are going to overcome your addictions, strive to find the proper balance between work, play, rest, exercise and leisure activities to produce optimal physical and psychological functioning. Improving your lifestyle hygiene will require lots of work. But if you are going to be strong enough, well rested enough, fresh enough to say no to the urge and temptation to your addiction, you must improve your diet, take exercise and get a good night's sleep.

Cultivate a sense of humour

Individuals who are well adjusted retain a sense of humour in order to enjoy life. Although they have concerns that guide them they avoid taking themselves, others or life too seriously. They work to maintain a hopeful and humorous attitude even when life is difficult and unrewarding.

Perhaps one of the greatest gifts nature has bestowed upon human beings is the ability to laugh at ourselves, others and world conditions. We urge you to cultivate your sense of humour. When you learn to laugh and see the humorous side of life you will be developing a wonderful coping skill. When you laugh your brain releases natural pain-killers called endorphins, and these are the truly healthy drugs to experience. Laughing at your own mistakes is a sign of having unconditional self-acceptance. A sense of humour can help you to tolerate discomfort and to persevere towards your goals in the face of setbacks.

A sense of humour can be developed. Study how others look at the funny side of life and experiment with developing such a point of view. Read books on the subject and learn how others cultivate humour. Learning to have a healthy sense of humour can be a vitally absorbing interest. So go ahead, learn to laugh, and maybe you will see how there are other highs in life besides those that are provided by drugs and alcohol, cigarettes and chocolate.

Adopting these fifteen principles is a life-long process and involves you identifying and disputing the irrational beliefs that block you from taking action derived from the principles.

Why not commit yourself to healthy living instead of to addicted living?

12

Deal with and learn from relapse

In this final chapter, we want to part company with you by giving you some final words of advice. Although we have said it many times before, self-change takes time and effort. Don't become discouraged because it is taking you time to learn how to implement our ideas. Implementing these ideas and overcoming your addiction is an ongoing effort. Changing involves trying again, again and again until you have practised the skills that allow you to think, feel and behave in a more effective way. If you are having some difficulty implementing our ideas, you are not failing – you are practising! Any effort you make to read about, try to use, and think about Rational Emotive Behaviour Therapy is part of your practice. So keep practising and in time you will overcome your addiction. As long as you keep challenging yourself and asking yourself how badly you want to overcome your addiction, you will keep creating the motivation to try once again. Keep focusing on what you will gain if you once and for all stay free, and you will stick with the task. You will be handsomely rewarded for fighting the discomfort of giving up. You will get your reward, but first you have to pay your dues!

Let's look at what you can do if you relapse after a period of abstinence and sobriety. First, acknowledge that you are back into your old habit. Think about the impact it has on your relationships with your family and friends. Think about the impact it has on your work performance and your career. Think about the danger you put yourself into when you are getting intoxicated (or drugged) and not in control. Focus on what you will gain if you stay with the abstinence effort! We acknowledge that all these addictions have a pleasant side to them. But we want you to acknowledge the pleasant side of *not* using them. Unless you keep in mind what you will gain by stopping once again, you just won't muster up the effort to put the beast of addiction back into hibernation!

Second, unconditionally accept yourself for having relapsed. Your human value is not measured by whether or not you stay free. You will have more pleasure in life if you stay free, but you won't be more worthwhile as a person.

Third, go back to the basics of Rational Emotive Behaviour Therapy. Remind yourself that you are largely responsible for your thoughts, feelings and drug use. Life and difficult people will give you an opportunity to get upset, but you make yourself upset! You choose to drink, smoke, binge or use drugs when you are tired, tempted and upset. Don't blame losing your job, a relationship break-up or any other negative event for choosing to cope with life with addiction. Identify what you told yourself just before you started looking for your cigarettes or booze. Write down your thoughts and dispute those absolute musts, have to's, demands and commands. You wanted to smoke or drink but you really didn't absolutely have to! Convince yourself of this. Dispute your irrational beliefs in whatever negative events you disturbed yourself about in the first place. Create rational coping statements and forcefully use them to control your behaviour. For example, tell yourself:

Rational Coping Statement 1
Relapse is a bad thing but I am not a bad person

Rational Coping Statement 2
The sooner I push myself to stop my addiction the better off I will be.

Rational Coping Statement 3
It is in my interests to focus on what I will gain by stopping my addiction.

Rational Coping Statement 4
I can stand the discomfort and frustration of pushing myself to think differently.

Rational Coping Statement 5
I can stand the discomfort of pushing myself to exercise to feel strong in my body and my mind.

Rational Coping Statement 6
I can stand the awkward feelings of trying out new activities when I have free time to replace my addiction.

Fourth, exercise, exercise, exercise! Once you relapse we bet you will either stop exercising or significantly reduce your exercising. Push yourself to start doing whatever kind of exercise you possibly can to break the ice and get back in the routine! Walk, run, cycle, swim, row, lift. Just break the ice and record your activity in your notebook. Try to exercise first thing in the morning so you will get to it before you start your old habit. Doing even the smallest amount of exercise will help you get back into the routine. Exercise every day if you can. When you have relapsed you really could use a life-raft, and daily exercise is just the life-raft we recommend. Walking is always the simplest and safest exercise. You don't need to be dressed in any special outfit to start walking.

Fifth, reach out for the support of a non-addict friend. Instead of listening to your cool friends who will urge you to drink, smoke, snort or party, have a discussion with a sensible, healthy individual. Don't ask for their pity. Ask them to help you identify and focus on what you will be gaining if you pick yourself up, dust yourself off and start pushing yourself to control your thoughts and behaviour. Ask them to help you identify all the good reasons for not going back to a drug-abusing, alcohol-dependent, addicted lifstyle. In order to fight the discomfort you feel when you are trying to stop using your substance of choice, you have to remain focused on how your life will improve. So get your healthy friends to help you keep in focus what you will gain if you stick with your ultimate goal of staying free!

Finally, look for ways to improve your use of Rational Emotive Behaviour Therapy. Generalization of skills means learning how to dispute your irrational beliefs to calm down in one situation, and then learning to use this self-help process consistently in many different situations. Generalization and further personal growth only come to those who continue to monitor their progress, and evaluate how to make more progress by identifying situations that need to be worked on and skills that need to be further practised and developed. Generalization of therapeutic progress only comes when you actively try to get better and better at using this approach to problems of daily living. The people who really do well with REBT are the people who try to use this powerful philosophy throughout the day, every day! So if you see yourself making some personal changes, don't become complacent. Old habits die hard and people do backslide! If you continue to use your REBT skills on a daily basis you stand a better chance of not backsliding and/or stopping backsliding at the initial stage of relapse. So don't rest on your therapeutic laurels. Don't assume that you have mastered REBT quickly. Keep identifying your self-defeating irrational beliefs, and once you have found them, dispute and change them. Release your new rational beliefs and use every opportunity to act in ways that are consistent with them. This way you will integrate them into your belief system. And don't forget that you can use the books that are listed in the preface to help you with problems that you are particularly prone to.

If you think and act rationally, you will increase your chances of staying sober and clear. It is a challenge, but one that, with persistence, you can rise to. Here's to a non-addicted life!

Index